Fiction Writing

A Practical Guide for Crafting Your First Novel

Lou Fetzer

Table of Contents

Introduction	3
Chapter 1: Getting Started—Overcoming the Blank Page	6
Understanding Common Fears and How to Conquer Them	7
Identifying Fear Triggers	7
Shifting Mindset	7
Taking Action	8
Celebrating Progress	9
Setting Up a Productive Writing Space	9
Choosing the Right Location	9
Organizing Writing Materials	10
Personalizing the Space	10
Minimizing Distractions	11
Ensuring Comfort	12
Finding Motivation	12
Establishing a Daily Writing Routine	12
Choosing the Right Time	13
Creating a Writing Schedule	13
Breaking Down Goals	14
Adjusting the Routine	14
Maintaining Motivation	15
Self-Care and Writing	15
Summary and Reflections	15
Chapter 2: Crafting Compelling Characters	17
Defining Character Archetypes and Roles	18
Developing Memorable Character Backstories	20
Crafting Backstories That Add Depth and Motivation	20
Practical Tips for Creating Effective Backstories	22
Examples in Literature and Film	22
Common Pitfalls to Avoid	23
How to Ensure Character Growth and Transformation	23
Final Thoughts	26

- Chapter 3: Building Immersive Worlds — 27
  - Different Approaches to World-Building — 27
  - The Importance of Setting in Shaping Narratives — 29
    - Setting as Character — 29
    - Creating Atmosphere — 30
    - Contextual Influence — 31
    - Time Period Significance — 31
  - Incorporating Sensory Details for Vivid Descriptions — 32
  - Concluding Thoughts — 34
- Chapter 4: Plotting Your Story—From Ideas to Outline — 36
  - Identifying Core Themes and Messages — 36
    - Defining Your Theme — 37
    - Connecting Themes to Character Arcs — 37
    - Utilizing Subthemes — 37
    - Evaluating Thematic Consistency — 38
  - Exploring Classical Plot Structures — 38
    - Three-Act Structure — 38
    - Hero's Journey — 39
    - Freytag's Pyramid — 40
    - Nonlinear Structures — 40
  - Techniques for Brainstorming and Organizing Ideas — 41
  - Bringing It All Together — 44
- Chapter 5: Writing Gripping Opening Scenes — 45
  - The Components of a Strong Opening Scene — 45
    - Establishing Tone and Style — 46
    - Introducing the Protagonist — 46
    - Setting the Scene With Sensory Details — 47
    - Setting Up the Inciting Incident — 48
    - Bringing It All Together — 48
  - How to Introduce Key Characters and Settings — 49
    - Showing Versus Telling — 49
    - Utilizing Dialogue Effectively — 50
    - Incorporating Backstory Naturally — 50
    - Creating a Vivid Setting Through Character Interaction — 51
    - Practical Guidelines and Examples — 51
    - Using Conflict and Stakes to Engage Readers — 52
  - Final Thoughts — 54
- Chapter 6: Maintaining Momentum—Writing the Middle — 56

Avoiding the Mid-Novel Slump	56
Developing Subplots That Enhance the Main Story	59
Keeping Character Development Consistent	61
Final Thoughts	64
Chapter 7: Crafting Satisfying Endings	65
Recognizing When to End Your Story	65
Resolving Main and Subplot Threads	68
Creating Emotional and Thematic Resonance	70
Summary and Reflections	72
Chapter 8: Self-Editing and Polishing Your Manuscript	74
Approaching Your Manuscript Objectively	74
Techniques for Line Editing and Copyediting	76
Using Beta Readers and Incorporating Feedback	78
Summary and Reflections	80
Chapter 9: Navigating the Publishing Landscape	82
Traditional vs. Self-Publishing Options	82
Writing an Effective Query Letter or Book Proposal	85
Understanding Contracts and Rights	87
Final Thoughts	90
Chapter 10: Staying Motivated and Productive	92
Setting Realistic Goals and Milestones	92
Balancing Writing With Other Responsibilities	95
Prioritization Techniques	96
Time Blocking	96
Mindful Multitasking	97
Flexibility and Adaptation	97
Celebrating Progress and Staying Inspired	98
Summary and Reflections	100
Conclusion	101
A Small Ask	104
References	105

Fiction Writing: A Practical Guide for Crafting Your First Novel

By Lou Fetzer

© Copyright 2024 - All rights reserved. One Jacked Monkey LLC.

The content contained within this book may not be reproduced, duplicated or transmitted without direct written permission from the author or the publisher.

Under no circumstances will any blame or legal responsibility be held against the publisher, or author, for any damages, reparation, or monetary loss due to the information contained within this book, either directly or indirectly.

Legal Notice:

This book is copyright protected. It is only for personal use. You cannot amend, distribute, sell, use, quote or paraphrase any part, or the content within this book, without the consent of the author or publisher.

Disclaimer Notice:

Please note the information contained within this document is for educational and entertainment purposes only. All effort has been executed to present accurate, up to date, reliable, complete information. No warranties of any kind are declared or implied. Readers acknowledge that the author is not engaged in the rendering of legal, financial, medical or professional advice. The content within this book has been derived from various sources. Please consult a licensed professional before attempting any techniques outlined in this book.

By reading this document, the reader agrees that under no circumstances is the author responsible for any losses, direct or indirect, that are incurred as a result of the use of the information contained within this document, including, but not limited to, errors, omissions, or inaccuracies.

Get up-to-date and relevant information in the world of writing and authorship, as well as, deals, discounts, and free advance access to books when you subscribe to our newsletter. Subscribe at **SelfPublishingNow.com.**

Introduction

Writing your first novel can feel like embarking on an uncharted adventure. You might be sitting at your desk right now, fingers hovering over the keyboard, wondering where to start. Take comfort in the fact that every great author started exactly where you are today—grappling with uncertainty and the thrill of potential. Your journey is not just about the end product—it's about embracing each moment as an opportunity for learning and growth. Every challenge you encounter along the way will become a stepping stone as you enhance your craft and shape your unique story.

With this mindset, consider the world around you through a lens of curiosity. Imagine walking through a bustling market where vibrant colors, lively conversations, and diverse aromas fill the air. In this setting, you might envision a character who finds solace in chaos, whose true story unfolds amid the vibrancy and energy of such surroundings. By cultivating curiosity, you open yourself up to endless possibilities and allow everyday experiences to spark brilliant ideas for your narratives.

As you continue on this journey, discovering your unique writing voice will be one of the most rewarding aspects. Your voice is the distinctive way you express thoughts and emotions on the page, and it will resonate deeply with your readers. Don't be afraid to experiment with different styles until you find what feels authentically yours. Let your words flow freely, capturing moments with vivid imagery and heartfelt emotion. For example, writing something like, "The moon hung low in the sky, its silvery light cascading over the rooftops like a gentle whisper, inviting secrets to dance in the night air," showcases your distinctive touch, breathing life into your scenes and characters.

To make this journey manageable, it's important to set achievable goals. Breaking your writing process into smaller, manageable milestones allows you to celebrate each victory along the way, no matter how small it may seem. For instance, setting a goal to write just 500 words a day might sound modest, but at the end of a month, you'll have a solid foundation of 15,000 words for your story. These small successes build momentum, keeping your motivation high and your spirits lifted.

The beauty of writing is that it's a continuous process of discovery and self-improvement. Embrace the highs and lows, knowing that each experience adds depth to your storytelling abilities. When you hit a roadblock, don't view it as a setback but rather as an opportunity to refine your skills. Maybe there's a plot point that's stubbornly elusive or a character whose development feels incomplete. Instead of getting frustrated, take a step back and observe what's happening. Often, these challenges push you to think creatively, leading to breakthroughs that enrich your narrative.

Think back to some of your favorite books and the authors behind them. Each of those writers faced their own set of uncertainties and obstacles. They persevered, constantly honing their craft and finding joy in the process. Today, you're beginning your own journey, equipped with your unique perspective and creativity. The path ahead is filled with unwritten stories waiting to be told, and you're the only one who can bring them to life.

As you embark on this adventure, remember to stay curious about the people, places, and interactions around you. Observing the world with a writer's eye transforms mundane moments into potential story gold. That quiet coffee shop conversation, the way sunlight filters through the trees, or the mix of emotions on a stranger's face—all of these can ignite new ideas and deepen your narratives. Foster a habit of writing down observations, thoughts, and whims. These snippets can become the seeds from which entire plots and characters grow.

Finding your voice is critical in making your stories resonate with readers on a deeper level. Authenticity speaks volumes and forms a connection between you and your audience. Play around with different tones, genres, and perspectives. You might start with gripping suspense and later find yourself drawn to heartfelt dramas or whimsical fantasies. There's no wrong pathway here; the goal is to discover the style where you feel most comfortable and genuine. Allow yourself to explore and write freely without the hindrance of self-judgment.

Achieving small goals along the way makes the seemingly monumental task of writing a book more approachable. Setting clear, intentional milestones allows you to track progress and savor each completed step. Whether it's dedicating time daily to writing, as mentioned earlier, outlining a chapter, or developing a character profile, each task you complete is a cause for celebration. Recognize and appreciate these achievements—they fuel your dedication and keep your passion burning bright.

Writing is indeed a journey—a personal odyssey where your imagination sets sail across uncharted waters. Along the way, you'll learn more about yourself and your capabilities, discovering the true essence of what drives your creative spirit. Accept the challenges as they come and relish the victories, both big and small. Before long, you'll find that you're not just writing a novel—you're crafting a testament to your perseverance, creativity, and growth.

Every word you write brings you closer to unlocking the full potential of your storytelling prowess. So, sit back, take a deep breath, and dive in with an open heart and an eager mind. Let your passion guide you through this incredible journey, and trust that, much like the authors you admire, you too will conquer the blank pages before you. The world is waiting to hear your story.

Chapter 1: Getting Started—Overcoming the Blank Page

Facing a blank page can be both exciting and intimidating for new writers. The sheer emptiness seems to taunt, bringing forth a wave of fears and anxieties that can freeze even the most passionate storyteller. These initial hurdles are common and often stem from self-doubt or a fear of criticism. Conquering the blank page is not merely about typing words onto it—it's about overcoming mental barriers and finding the courage to start your writing journey.

In this chapter, you will find practical guidance on how to dismantle these fears and create an environment conducive to consistent writing. We'll explore strategies for identifying what triggers your anxiety and methods for shifting your mindset to view writing as a journey rather than a task requiring perfection. You'll learn how to set up a productive writing space, establish a manageable writing routine, and celebrate small victories along the way. By the end of this chapter, you'll have a toolkit of techniques to help you confidently face the blank page and begin crafting your stories.

As you begin this journey, the strategies in this chapter will help you overcome early obstacles and build momentum. These foundational techniques are essential for establishing a consistent writing routine and setting yourself up for success. Later, in Chapter 10, we'll revisit some of these ideas and delve deeper into additional tools and strategies to keep you motivated and productive as you move closer to completing your manuscript.

Understanding Common Fears and How to Conquer Them

Many novice writers find themselves frozen in place by a sense of fear and anxiety when faced with a blank page. These emotions are entirely normal and affect writers of all levels. However, for those just starting out, these feelings can be particularly paralyzing. This section aims to address the fears that often block new writers and provide actionable strategies to overcome them.

Identifying Fear Triggers

Understanding what triggers your fear is the first step in overcoming it. Common fears include the fear of failure and the fear of criticism. The fear of failure might stem from a belief that you won't be able to translate your ideas into compelling writing, while the fear of criticism often arises from worries about how others will perceive your work. Recognizing these fears is crucial because awareness allows you to prepare and strategize against them.

For example, many writers fear that their work isn't good enough and worry about negative feedback. This fear can stop you before you even begin. It's important to know that every writer faces these doubts. If you acknowledge these fears, you can start to address them. Take a moment to write down specific scenarios or thoughts that trigger your fear of writing. Is it opening a blank document or the thought of sharing your work with someone else? Jotting these triggers down can help you understand your fear better.

Shifting Mindset

Changing your mindset about writing and failure can significantly impact your ability to overcome fear. Instead of viewing writing as a task where perfection is the goal, consider adopting a mindset focused on growth and exploration. Writing is a journey, not a destination. Each word you write brings you closer to improving your craft.

One effective way to shift your mindset is to embrace the concept of "writing scared" (Weiland, 2019). This involves acknowledging that fear is part of the process and using it as a motivator rather than a barrier. When fear rears its head, see it as a sign that you're pushing your boundaries and growing as a writer. Write about your fears, make them part of your story, and let them guide you toward deeper and more authentic writing.

Another method to change your perspective is to practice gratitude for the opportunity to write. Think about how writing contributes to your personal growth and allows you to express yourself creatively. By focusing on the positives, you can reduce the power that fear holds over you.

Taking Action

Overcoming fear requires taking concrete steps, no matter how small they may seem. Setting manageable, low-commitment goals can help build momentum. For instance, start by committing to writing for just 10 minutes a day. This small step can gradually ease you into a regular writing habit without overwhelming you.

Breaking your writing tasks into smaller sections can also make them seem less daunting. Instead of aiming to finish an entire chapter in one sitting, break it down into paragraphs or scenes. This approach reduces the pressure and makes the task more approachable.

The fear-setting method (*Dealing W ith and Overcoming* , n.d.) is another useful technique. Start by defining your fears—list them out honestly. Next, think of ways to prevent these fears from coming true. For instance, if you're afraid of writer's block, set aside time for brainstorming before you start writing. Finally, consider the benefits of taking action despite your fears. What will you gain if you push through? This could be anything from completing a draft to gaining new writing skills.

Celebrating Progress

Recognizing and celebrating small victories is essential for reinforcing positive behavior. Each step forward, no matter how minor, is progress and should be acknowledged. Did you manage to write for 10 minutes today? Celebrate that achievement. Did you finish a paragraph or a page? Give yourself credit for putting in the work.

Keeping a journal of your accomplishments, no matter how small, can serve as a motivational tool. When you look back and see the progress you've made, you'll feel encouraged to keep moving forward. Another way to celebrate progress is to share your achievements with a supportive community. Whether it's an online forum or a local writing group, having others recognize your efforts can provide additional motivation.

Engaging in mini-rewards can also reinforce positive behavior. Treat yourself to something enjoyable when you reach a milestone. It could be a favorite snack, a walk outside, or a short break to watch a funny video. These rewards make the writing process more enjoyable and give you something to look forward to.

Setting Up a Productive Writing Space

Creating a conducive writing environment is essential for unleashing your creative potential and maintaining focus. The right setting can significantly influence the quality of your work and your ability to sustain long writing sessions. Let's explore some practical guidelines to help you create an ideal writing space.

Choosing the Right Location

Selecting the perfect spot for your writing endeavors is more important than you might think. An effective writing location should minimize distractions and foster concentration. Start by identifying spaces in your home where interruptions are least likely to occur. It could be a quiet corner of your bedroom, a small home office, or even a cozy spot in the living room. The aim is to find a place that feels comfortable yet isolated enough to keep household distractions at bay.

Consider the lighting in your chosen space. Natural light can be incredibly invigorating, so if possible, position your desk near a window. However, ensure that the light is not too direct, which could cause glare on your screen or paper. Complement natural light with good-quality artificial lighting to avoid straining your eyes during late-night writing sessions.

Organizing Writing Materials

A clutter-free workspace is not just aesthetically pleasing but also crucial for maintaining focus. Disorganization can lead to constant interruptions as you search for materials, breaking your writing flow and causing frustration. Begin by gathering all the essential tools you'll need: notebooks, pens, reference books, and your computer. Invest in organizers such as desk trays, pen holders, and shelves to keep everything within easy reach.

Labeling folders and keeping digital files organized can also save time and reduce stress. Create specific folders for drafts, research, and notes. Regularly sort through these folders to discard outdated or irrelevant material. The goal is to create an environment where you can effortlessly find what you need when you need it.

One often overlooked aspect is keeping your digital workspace tidy as well. Close unnecessary tabs and apps to eliminate digital clutter. Tools like *Trello* or *Evernote* can help you organize tasks and ideas efficiently.

Personalizing the Space

Your writing space should be a reflection of your personality and creativity. Personalizing your area can make it more inviting and stimulating. Introduce elements that inspire you, such as artwork, photographs, or motivational quotes. These items can serve as visual stimuli that spark creativity whenever you glance at them.

Plants are another excellent addition. Not only do they enhance the aesthetics of your space, but studies have also shown that having plants around can reduce stress and increase productivity. Choose low-maintenance plants like succulents or snake plants if you're new to caring for them.

Moreover, consider the significance of colors in your workspace. Different colors can evoke different moods. While blue can be calming and boost productivity, red might inspire passion and energy. Experiment with hues to find what resonates best with your writing style.

Minimizing Distractions

Even the most perfectly organized and personalized space can be rendered ineffective by distractions. Knowing how to mitigate interruptions is key to maintaining a steady writing routine. One powerful strategy is to set specific "do not disturb" times. Inform family members or roommates about your writing schedule and request that they avoid interrupting you during those periods.

Utilizing tools such as website blockers can also help maintain focus. Applications like *Cold Turkey* or *Freedom* can block distracting websites and apps during your designated writing hours, allowing you to concentrate fully on your work.

Consider creating a ritual to signal the start and end of your writing sessions. This might involve dimming the lights, playing a particular type of music, or even brewing a cup of tea. Such routines can prepare your mind to switch into writing mode and create a mental barrier against distractions.

If noise is a significant issue, noise-canceling headphones or white noise machines can be invaluable. Music can also serve as a beneficial tool, provided it doesn't distract you. Instrumental tracks or nature sounds often work well for many writers.

Ensuring Comfort

Investing in a comfortable chair is essential for long writing sessions. Choose one that supports your back and encourages good posture to prevent discomfort and fatigue. Pair this with a desk set at the right height to avoid straining your neck, shoulders, or wrists. Additionally, keep comfort items nearby, such as a cozy blanket, a favorite mug for your coffee or tea, and snacks to keep you energized. These personal touches not only add to your physical comfort but also create a welcoming atmosphere that can make your writing sessions more enjoyable and productive.

Finding Motivation

An inspiration board can be a powerful tool for sparking creativity and maintaining motivation. By setting up a space where you can pin ideas, images, and quotes, you create a visual representation of your thoughts and goals. This board can serve as a constant source of inspiration, helping you overcome writer's block and stay focused on your projects. Whether it's pictures that evoke a certain mood, quotes from your favorite authors, or sketches of characters and settings, an inspiration board brings your creative vision to life. It serves as a dynamic and evolving resource that keeps your ideas organized and your enthusiasm for writing high.

Establishing a Daily Writing Routine

Consistency in writing is key to developing your craft and producing quality work. Establishing a daily routine can help ensure that writing becomes a regular part of your life rather than something you do sporadically. Below are some strategies to help you establish and maintain a consistent writing practice.

Choosing the Right Time

Everyone has different energy levels and peak productivity times, so it's essential to experiment with various times throughout the day and find what works best for you. Some writers find the tranquil afternoon hours, with soft light filtering through the windows, ideal for writing. Even dusk, with its calm and reflective atmosphere, can inspire creativity as the day turns to night. By trying out different times, you can discover when you're most creative and productive.

Consider keeping a journal to track your writing sessions and note how you feel at different times. This can provide insights into when your mind and body are most receptive to the task. Once you've identified an ideal time, aim to stick with it consistently. The goal is to make this time a nonnegotiable part of your daily routine.

Creating a Writing Schedule

Building a consistent writing schedule involves more than just selecting a good time of day. It also requires a commitment to showing up regularly. One effective way to ensure consistency is by using calendars or planners to block out dedicated writing time. Mark these slots as "writing appointments" and treat them with the same respect as any other important meeting.

Set realistic expectations for how much time you can devote to writing each day. It's better to start small—perhaps 30 minutes a day—and gradually increase as you become more comfortable. Overcommitting can lead to burnout and frustration, making it harder to maintain consistency in the long run.

Using digital tools like *Google Calendar* or dedicated writing apps can help you keep track of your schedule. Setting reminders can ensure you don't forget or skip your writing time. The key is to create a habit of sitting down to write at the same time every day until it becomes second nature.

Breaking Down Goals

Setting achievable writing goals is another crucial aspect of maintaining consistency. Goals give you something concrete to work toward and can keep you motivated even on days when inspiration is lacking. Start by defining what you want to achieve in your writing sessions. This could be a word count target, completing a chapter, or finishing a specific section of your project.

For example, you might set a goal of writing 500 words per day or finishing one chapter per week. These small, manageable targets can add up over time and lead to significant progress. Breaking down larger projects into smaller tasks makes them less daunting and more attainable.

Tracking your progress can also provide a sense of accomplishment and motivate you to keep going. Use a journal or an app to record your daily word count, the chapters you've completed, or other milestones. Reflecting on your progress reinforces positive behavior and helps you see how far you've come.

Adjusting the Routine

While consistency is important, flexibility is equally crucial. Life is unpredictable, and there will be days when sticking to your routine is challenging. It's essential to adapt and adjust your writing schedule to accommodate changes and responsibilities.

If you miss a scheduled session, don't be too hard on yourself. Instead, look for ways to make up for it. Perhaps you can write a bit more the next day or find a different time slot. The goal is to stay committed to your overall writing habit without being rigid.

Flexibility also means being open to changing your routine if it's not working. If you find that your chosen time isn't as productive as you hoped, don't hesitate to experiment with new times or methods. The key is to find a balance between structure and adaptability.

Maintaining Motivation

Staying motivated is a common challenge for many writers. One way to keep motivation high is by rewarding yourself for meeting your writing goals. Rewards can be simple, like taking a break, enjoying a treat, or doing something you love after a successful writing session. Positive reinforcement encourages you to continue putting in the effort.

Joining writing groups or communities can also provide motivation and accountability. Sharing your goals with others and receiving feedback can be incredibly encouraging. Knowing that others expect to see your work can push you to stay consistent.

Additionally, finding a dedicated writing space can enhance focus and productivity. A quiet, organized area reserved solely for writing can help you get into the right mindset. Personalize this space with items that inspire you, such as artwork, plants, or motivational quotes.

Self-Care and Writing

Taking care of yourself physically and mentally is essential for sustaining a writing practice. Ensure you're getting enough sleep, eating well, and engaging in activities that bring you joy. Managing stress and anxiety is also crucial, as these can hinder your ability to write.

Incorporate self-care routines into your daily schedule to maintain a healthy balance. This might include exercise, meditation, or spending time with loved ones. When you prioritize your well-being, you're better equipped to tackle your writing goals.

Summary and Reflections

In this chapter, we've delved into the common fears that often hold new writers back and explored practical strategies to address them.

We've identified specific triggers like fear of failure and criticism and discussed how changing your mindset can be a powerful tool in overcoming these anxieties. By embracing concepts like "writing scared" and practicing gratitude, you can start viewing writing as a journey of growth rather than a quest for perfection.

Additionally, we've highlighted the importance of taking concrete steps to establish a productive writing routine and creating a supportive environment. Setting small, manageable goals and celebrating each milestone can build momentum and confidence. Remember, every writer faces moments of doubt, but with persistence and the right strategies, you can conquer your fears and continue developing your craft. Keep pushing forward, one word at a time, and cherish the progress you make along the way.

Chapter 2: Crafting Compelling Characters

Crafting compelling characters is at the heart of any great story. Whether you're writing a novel, short story, or screenplay, your characters are what will draw readers in and keep them engaged. A well-developed character resonates with readers, giving them someone to root for or against, someone they can see parts of themselves in, or someone who opens their eyes to new perspectives. It's not just about having an interesting plot—it's about populating that plot with characters who feel real, each with their own desires, fears, and complexities.

In this chapter, we delve into the art and science of creating multidimensional characters. We'll start by exploring classic character archetypes—such as the Hero, the Mentor, and the Shadow—and how these can serve as foundational models. But remember, sticking strictly to these archetypes can make your characters predictable. That's why we'll also discuss how to add unique traits and backstories to breathe fresh life into these roles, making your characters more relatable and engaging.

Additionally, we'll examine the roles different characters play within a narrative, from protagonists to antagonists to supporting characters, and how to use these roles effectively to shape your story. There are strategies like introducing unique twists and employing ensemble casts that can add layers of complexity and originality to your work. By the end of this chapter, you'll have a toolkit full of techniques to craft compelling characters that will captivate your readers.

Defining Character Archetypes and Roles

When it comes to crafting compelling characters, understanding archetypes is a valuable starting point. Archetypes are classic character models that exist across various stories and cultures. Recognizable ones like the Hero, Mentor, and Shadow mentioned earlier streamline character development by providing a foundation upon which you can build. For instance, the Hero often embodies qualities like courage and determination. Think of protagonists such as Frodo from *The Lord of the Rings* or Katniss Everdeen from *The Hunger Games* . These characters resonate with readers because their core traits align with the heroic archetype.

However, if you do nothing but adhere to these classic models, your characters can feel predictable. That's where individual characteristics come in. By layering unique traits and backstories onto these traditional frameworks, you can breathe fresh life into conventional roles. Imagine a Mentor who has a dark past that contradicts their wise exterior or a Hero who suffers from crippling self-doubt. These nuances add depth and complexity, making the characters more relatable and engaging.

Moving on to the role of characters in the narrative, it's essential to understand the functions of protagonists, antagonists, and supporting characters. The protagonist is the central figure around whom the story revolves. They drive the plot forward through their actions and decisions. Take Harry Potter, for example: His journey from an ordinary boy to a powerful wizard propels the entire series.

On the flip side, the antagonist creates conflict, challenging the protagonist and adding tension to the story. Whether it's an evil sorcerer like Voldemort or a more abstract force like societal norms, antagonists are crucial for highlighting the protagonist's strengths and weaknesses. Supporting characters also play pivotal roles by influencing the protagonist's journey with their advice, friendships, or opposition. Hermione Granger and Ron Weasley are prime examples of supporting characters who enrich Harry Potter's story, offering both aid and emotional depth.

Creating unique twists is another way to keep readers hooked. Subverting or blending archetypes not only adds originality but also prevents your characters from becoming clichés. Consider how George R.R. Martin's (1996–2011) Game of Thrones series turns archetypes on their heads. Characters like Arya Stark defy traditional gender roles, while Tyrion Lannister combines elements of the Trickster and Sage archetypes, making him unpredictable and intriguing.

By deliberately choosing to subvert expectations, you can surprise and engage your audience. A villain turned hero or a seemingly insignificant side character who becomes central to the plot can add layers of complexity and keep readers invested. This technique encourages readers to rethink their preconceived notions about character roles and can lead to more dynamic storytelling.

Another strategy to enhance your narrative is utilizing ensemble casts. An ensemble cast allows you to introduce multiple viewpoints and experiences, enriching the story with diverse perspectives. This approach works particularly well in genres like fantasy, science fiction, and drama. Ensemble casts offer various characters that readers can connect with, each adding their own flavor to the narrative.

For instance, J.K. Rowling's Harry Potter series doesn't just focus on Harry. Characters like Hermione, Ron, Dumbledore, and even lesser-known figures like Neville Longbottom contribute to the overall storyline, each bringing their unique challenges and growth arcs. This variety makes the world more immersive and complex.

When creating an ensemble cast, it's important to ensure that each character has a distinct voice and personality. This diversity allows for richer interactions and conflicts, making the narrative more engaging. For example, the television show *Friends* is successful not just because of its humor but because each character—Ross, Rachel, Monica, Chandler, Joey, and Phoebe—brings something different to the table. Their unique traits and backgrounds create a tapestry of interconnected lives that viewers find hard to resist.

In summary, identifying different character types and their purposes can significantly improve your storytelling.

Understanding classic archetypes provides a strong foundation, while adding individual traits brings depth and relatability. Knowing the roles characters play within the narrative helps structure your story effectively. Creating unique twists keeps readers engaged and employing an ensemble cast introduces varied perspectives that enrich the overall experience.

Developing Memorable Character Backstories

Crafting Backstories That Add Depth and Motivation

Crafting compelling characters involves more than just defining their physical appearance or quirks. One of the most crucial aspects is developing a backstory that adds depth and motivation, making characters feel real and relatable to readers. This subpoint will guide you on how to create such backstories, which are divided into several key areas.

Importance of Backstory

A character's past profoundly influences their present actions and motivations. Just as our personal histories shape who we are today, a well-developed backstory can give a character realistic flaws, strengths, fears, and desires. Consider someone who grew up in a war zone—their experiences can manifest as hyper-vigilance or a strong desire for peace. By understanding this, writers can create characters whose actions and decisions are consistent and believable.

Building Compelling Histories

Creating detailed backstories might seem daunting, but there are techniques that can make this process manageable and even fun. One effective method is conducting character interviews. Imagine sitting down with your character and asking them questions about their past. What was their childhood like? Who were their closest friends? What significant events shaped their worldview? Another useful technique is creating timelines that map out critical moments in a character's life. This provides a visual representation of their history and helps ensure consistency throughout your story.

Balancing Relevance and Mystery

While it's essential to develop a thorough backstory, overwhelming readers with too much information at once can be counterproductive. A better approach is to gradually reveal the backstory. Dropping hints and relevant details at appropriate moments can maintain suspense and keep readers engaged. For instance, instead of explaining a character's traumatic childhood in one go, you could show how they react in certain situations, letting readers infer the underlying causes over time. This method keeps the narrative intriguing and prevents it from becoming bogged down by exposition (Martin, 2023).

Using Backstory to Enhance Themes

Another powerful use of backstory is to tie it to the overarching themes of your narrative. If your story explores themes of redemption, the backstory of a character seeking forgiveness allows for a deeper exploration of this theme. This connection enriches both the character and the overall story, providing a cohesive reading experience. For instance, in George Orwell's (1949) *1984*, Winston Smith's rebellious tendencies are deeply rooted in his past, which aligns with the book's theme of resisting oppressive regimes.

Practical Tips for Creating Effective Backstories

- **Introduce the backstory gradually.** Instead of dumping all the information at once, reveal it bit by bit. Allow readers to piece together the character's history.
- **Ensure relevance.** Every element of the backstory should serve a purpose, whether it's to deepen character development or move the plot forward.
- **Balance exposition with action.** Show backstory through actions, dialogue, and interactions rather than telling it outright. This makes the story more engaging (Feccomandi, 2024).
- **Leave room for interpretation.** Allow readers to draw their own conclusions about the backstory. This promotes active engagement and makes the story more immersive.
- **Understand character motivations.** Know what drives your characters and how their past influences their current goals and behaviors.

By incorporating these tips, you can craft backstories that add substantial depth to your characters, making them more relatable and engaging for your readers.

Examples in Literature and Film

To understand the narrative potential of backstory, let's consider some examples. In J.K. Rowling's (1997–2007) Harry Potter series, Severus Snape's complex backstory is gradually unveiled, transforming him from a seemingly antagonistic figure into a tragic hero. Understanding his past motivations adds layers to his character and deepens readers' emotional investment. Similarly, in Christopher Nolan's film *The Dark Knight* , Batman's traumatic childhood experiences are revealed through flashbacks and dialogue (2008). These revelations humanize the character and make his vigilante efforts more compelling.

Common Pitfalls to Avoid

While crafting backstories, be cautious of common pitfalls. Avoid overwhelming readers with an excessive information dump. Focus on including relevant details that contribute to the main narrative. Steer clear of heavy exposition by integrating backstory naturally into the plot.

How to Ensure Character Growth and Transformation

Highlighting the significance of character arcs and personal growth throughout a story is pivotal to creating compelling characters that resonate with readers. Understanding how characters evolve, interact with conflicts, set goals, and form relationships can transform a narrative into a memorable journey. This section will delve into the various aspects of character arcs, their importance, and effective ways to showcase growth.

Understanding character arcs forms the foundation of meaningful storytelling. There are primarily three types: static, dynamic, and flat arcs. A static arc involves a character who remains unchanged throughout the story. Typically, these characters are steadfast in their beliefs and serve as constants in an ever-changing plot. Dynamic arcs depict characters who undergo significant transformation. These arcs are often the most engaging, as they show personal growth influenced by the events of the narrative. Lastly, flat arcs represent characters who know the truth from the beginning and work to change the world around them by spreading that truth. Each type of arc serves different purposes in storytelling but collectively illustrates the broad spectrum of personal journeys characters can undertake.

Conflict plays a crucial role in driving character growth. External and internal conflicts challenge a character's core beliefs and reveal their true traits. External conflicts are those arising from outside forces—whether other characters, societal structures, or environmental factors. Internal conflicts, however, deal with a character's psychological struggles and inner turmoil. Man vs. self is the most archetypal of all stories because it encapsulates this internal conflict (Weiland, 2019a). The tug-of-war between a character's wants and needs propels them toward self-discovery and growth. Whether a character faces an external antagonist or battles internal fears and doubts, overcoming these challenges leads to profound personal development.

Establishing clear goals and motivations for characters is essential. When characters have defined objectives, they create tension and drive the narrative forward. Goals act as catalysts for action and transformation, often leading characters out of their comfort zones and pushing them to grow. Motivations explain why characters pursue specific goals, adding depth and relatability. If a character wishes to avenge a loved one, their goal may propel them into dangerous situations, revealing their bravery and vulnerability along the way. Clear goals and strong motivations not only make characters more engaging but also provide a roadmap for their arcs, ensuring consistent and logical progression.

Another essential element in reinforcing character growth is through relationships with secondary characters. These relationships shape development and add layers to the protagonist's journey. Interactions with friends, mentors, rivals, and love interests can highlight different facets of a character's personality and influence their path. For instance, a mentor might challenge the protagonist's worldview, prompting a critical turning point in their arc. Conversely, a rival could push the protagonist to confront their limits and strive for greatness. Relationships act as mirrors, reflecting back the character's flaws, strengths, and potential for growth.

Let's dive deeper into each aspect to exemplify their importance and implementation.

Static arcs might seem less dynamic, but they are fundamental in certain narratives. Take Sherlock Holmes as an example—a character whose unwavering brilliance and unique worldview remain constant (Doyle, 2003). Sherlock's static arc serves to anchor the story, allowing the plot and other characters to spiral around his steady core. His lack of change highlights the transformation occurring within those he interacts with, making his constancy a powerful narrative tool.

Dynamic arcs are perhaps the most beloved in fiction. Characters like Harry Potter encapsulate the essence of dynamic arcs. From a naïve boy living under the staircase to a self-sacrificing hero battling dark forces, Harry's growth is gradual and well-defined. Each book in the series represents a step in his journey, molded by triumphs, losses, friendships, and adversities. His arc is a testament to how experiences and conflicts shape identity over time (Rowling, 1997–2007).

Flat arcs, though less common, offer unique opportunities for storytelling. Consider Katniss Everdeen from The Hunger Games series. From the outset, Katniss holds firm beliefs about survival, sacrifice, and justice. Her arc doesn't center on her changing these beliefs but rather on challenging and transforming the corrupt society she lives in. Through her steadfastness, she influences others and initiates broader changes in her world (Collins, 2008–2010).

External and internal conflicts are indispensable narrative devices. In J.R.R. Tolkien's (1954–1955) The Lord of the Rings series, Frodo Baggins faces external conflicts such as battles against orcs and the treacherous journey to Mount Doom. Simultaneously, he grapples with the internal conflict of bearing the corrupting influence of the One Ring. Such duality of conflict deepens his character, illustrating courage, resilience, and vulnerability.

Motivations and goals imbue characters with purpose. In *Breaking Bad* , Walter White's transformation from a meek chemistry teacher to a ruthless drug lord is driven by his initial goal to secure his family's financial future. However, as the series progresses, his motivations become entangled with pride, power, and ego, leading to complex and destructive outcomes (Gilligan, 2008–2013). Defining clear goals and motivations ensures characters act consistently and their arcs remain believable.

Relationships reinforce character growth poignantly. In *To Kill a Mockingbird* , Scout Finch's interactions with her father, Atticus, are instrumental (Lee, 1960). Atticus's wisdom and moral integrity guide Scout's understanding of justice and empathy. Similarly, Boo Radley's eventual friendship with Scout teaches her about compassion and human complexity, marking her emotional and moral growth throughout the novel.

Final Thoughts

To wrap up, this chapter has taken you through the essentials of creating multidimensional characters that truly resonate with readers. We've explored the importance of understanding character archetypes and roles, emphasizing how adding unique traits can transform conventional models into engaging personalities. By subverting expectations and utilizing ensemble casts, you can keep your audience hooked and invested in your story. Each character should bring their own flavor to the narrative, contributing to a richer, more immersive experience.

Remember, memorable characters often stem from well-crafted backstories that offer depth and motivation. These histories shape your character's actions, flaws, and strengths, making them relatable and real. Revealing the backstory gradually while tying it to the story's themes can maintain reader interest and add layers to your plot. Whether through dramatic transformation or steadfast constancy, character growth is key to a compelling story. With these tools in your arsenal, you're well on your way to creating characters that will captivate and linger in the minds of your readers.

Chapter 3: Building Immersive Worlds

Building immersive worlds is a captivating journey that transforms your story into a vivid experience. Imagine wandering through a bustling medieval marketplace, hearing the clink of blacksmiths at work and smelling fresh bread from nearby stalls. The charm of world-building lies in its power to draw readers deeply into these richly crafted settings, letting them see, hear, and feel every detail. As a writer, constructing such detailed environments is more than just creating a backdrop; it's about developing an engaging universe where your characters can come alive and your plot can unfold seamlessly.

This chapter will walk you through various approaches to world-building, ensuring you find methods that resonate with your unique style. You'll explore historical research to give authenticity to your settings, learn to balance fantasy elements with realism, and understand modular techniques that keep your world adaptable as your story evolves. Additionally, we'll delve into collaborative efforts that can enrich your creative process by incorporating multiple perspectives. Each approach offers tools and insights to help you create a believable, captivating world that enhances your narrative and draws readers in from the very first page.

Different Approaches to World-Building

To explore various methods of creating fictional worlds, it's essential to discover an approach that resonates with your style. World-building is a fundamental aspect of storytelling that can greatly enhance the reader's experience by providing a rich and immersive setting. From historical research to balancing fantasy and realism, modular world-building, and collaborative efforts, there are several methods that you can employ to bring your worlds to life.

Firstly, historical research can be a powerful tool when you are looking to build authentic and believable worlds. By basing a fictional world on real historical events, you can lend a sense of authenticity and richness to your stories. For example, the complexities of political intrigue during the Renaissance or the societal structures of ancient civilizations can provide a robust framework for a fictional world. Understanding historical contexts can help in building cohesive and realistic settings, where the actions and customs of characters are consistent with the time period being depicted. Integrating accurate details such as clothing, architecture, and social norms can further enhance reader immersion and make the fictional setting come alive. Researching diverse cultures provides rich material for unique settings and can inspire fresh and innovative world-building ideas.

While historical research grounds a story in reality, the balance between fantasy and realism is another critical aspect of world-building. Writers often face the challenge of maintaining coherence while introducing fantastical elements. Establishing rules for fantasy worlds is crucial for maintaining consistency. Whether it's the way magic operates or the characteristics of mythical creatures, having defined parameters helps to create a believable universe. For instance, if a world has dragons, explaining their biology, habitat, and interaction with humans can add depth and credibility. At the same time, incorporating realistic elements, such as natural landscapes or human emotions, allows readers to connect more deeply with the narrative. The interplay between the imaginative and the realistic creates a dynamic and engaging world where the extraordinary feels anchored in the possible.

Modular world-building can be another effective approach for you. This method involves creating foundational components that can be combined flexibly, allowing for adaptable storytelling as the plot evolves. You can focus on core elements first, gradually expanding the universe. For example, starting with a well-defined city and its key locations enables you to elaborate on neighboring regions and the larger world as the story progresses. This approach not only makes the world-building process more manageable but also encourages innovation, as you can rearrange components for unique outcomes. Modular world-building is particularly useful for long-term projects where the narrative might shift directions based on character development or plot twists. It provides a strong yet flexible foundation that can accommodate the evolving needs of the story.

Collaborative world-building is another valuable method, especially if you are seeking to broaden your perspectives and deepen the details of your worlds. Engaging with other writers for joint creation can lead to richer and more diverse settings. Sharing ideas fosters a broader perspective, allowing each contributor to bring their unique insights and creativity to the table. This collective effort can result in a more nuanced and layered world, filled with varied cultural, social, and political structures. Collaborative world-building also provides opportunities for peer feedback, which can refine and enhance the created world. Feedback from peers can highlight inconsistencies or suggest enhancements that you might have overlooked, leading to a more polished and immersive setting. Collaborations can inspire novel concepts beyond what you envisioned, adding unexpected dimensions to the fictional world.

The Importance of Setting in Shaping Narratives

Imagine stepping into a dimly lit alley, the narrow passage cluttered with discarded newspapers fluttering in an eerie breeze. The setting here isn't just a backdrop—it's alive, breathing, and integral to shaping the drama that unfolds. When crafting a story, treating the environment as an essential component rather than mere scenery can profoundly influence character actions and plot developments.

Setting as Character

A well-defined setting has the power to act almost like another character in your narrative. Think of it as more than just where the story transpires; consider how this place impacts and interacts with your characters. For instance, in *Wuthering Heights* by Emily Brontë (1847), the moors aren't just the locale but an extension of the characters' turbulent emotions. The desolate, rugged landscape mirrors Heathcliff's inner turmoil and passion. Similarly, in Agatha Christie's (1964) *A Caribbean Mystery* , the sunny beach resort lulls readers into a false sense of security before the murder shakes everything up, making the shock even more jarring. Here, the environment becomes part of the narrative's fabric, shaping how events unfold and how characters react.

Creating Atmosphere

T he atmosphere of a setting can evoke specific emotions in readers, enhancing their engagement with the story. Atmospheric descriptions are crucial in eliciting emotional responses such as tension, joy, or dread. For example, describing a scene set in an abandoned house with creaking floors, flickering lights, and distant whispers can create a mood of suspense and fear. In contrast, a scene set on a vibrant, sun-drenched coast with the sound of waves gently lapping can evoke relaxation and warmth.

Balancing light, color, and sound in your descriptions can intensify these emotions. A morning scene bathed in golden sunlight with birds chirping can fill readers with hope and cheeriness. Conversely, a forest at twilight with long shadows and rustling leaves can spark unease or apprehension. By carefully crafting these sensory details, you can make your world feel immersive and vividly real.

Atmospheric settings also have the power to foreshadow events. A sudden storm in the midst of calm weather might hint at impending conflict or disaster, making the narrative appear interconnected and fluid. Imagine a romance blooming under cherry blossoms only for petals to fall like tears during a heartbreak scene—such imagery ties the emotional arcs to the physical world seamlessly.

Contextual Influence

Cultural, social, and political backgrounds deeply influence the storyline and character motivations. They shape the world your characters inhabit, dictating societal norms, conflicts, and challenges they face. For example, consider a story set in 18th century England, where strict social hierarchies could thwart a love affair between different classes, or a dystopian future where totalitarian regimes enforce harsh laws affecting every aspect of daily life.

These contexts provide rich ground for external conflicts and deepen plot complexity. An immigrant family struggling to adapt to a foreign land offers not just a personal journey but insights into broader cultural clashes and integration challenges. Or a rebellion against oppressive rule can explore themes of freedom, identity, and sacrifice, making the setting integral to the narrative's core message.

Understanding these contexts enables you as a writer to weave intricate plots that resonate on multiple levels, engaging readers beyond the surface events. It's about drawing from real-life parallels and imbuing your world with verisimilitude, making it both relatable and thought-provoking.

Time Period Significance

The time period in which your story is set greatly influences the technology, language, and behavior of the characters. For instance, a tale set in medieval times will differ drastically from one in a futuristic sci-fi universe. The technology available to characters dictates their actions and limitations—sending a letter via horseback versus instant messaging changes the pacing and tension in communication dramatically.

Exploring historical events as plot catalysts can add tension and depth to your story. A narrative set during World War II, for instance, benefits from historical tensions, providing a backdrop enriched with stakes and urgency. Historical contexts offer unique pressures and opportunities for characters to grow and face monumental choices shaped by the era's distinct challenges.

Furthermore, understanding societal shifts within those periods can enhance character interactions. Characters in Victorian England adhere to different social mores compared to contemporary settings. This knowledge allows you to present conflicts that feel authentic and grounded in their respective timelines, offering readers a nuanced experience.

Incorporating Sensory Details for Vivid Descriptions

Using sensory details is a powerful way to create vivid, immersive worlds that draw readers into your story. By appealing to the senses—sight, sound, smell, touch, and taste—you can paint a picture so real that readers feel as though they are stepping into your fictional universe. This technique not only enhances the setting but also deepens reader engagement.

Let's start with the Five Senses Framework. Utilizing all five senses in your descriptions can make scenes come alive. Visual elements are often the first detail we think of; describing what a character sees can set the foundation for an engaging scene. For instance, instead of simply stating, "The forest was dense," you might describe, "Tall pine trees stood like sentinels, their dark green needles blotting out the sun." This creates a visual image that gives readers a clearer picture of the setting.

Next, let's discuss the importance of sound. The auditory details, such as the melody of a bird's song or the crunch of leaves underfoot, can add another layer to the reader's experience. Imagine a quiet village; the silence can be punctuated by distant church bells or the chatter of locals at the market, each sound contributing to the atmosphere.

Smell is a potent yet often underutilized sense in writing. The scent of fresh-baked bread wafting through the air can evoke comfort and warmth, while the stench of decaying leaves might instill a sense of unease. Smells can trigger memories and emotions, making descriptions more evocative.

Touch involves the tactile sensations experienced by characters. Describing the texture of objects, whether it's the rough bark of a tree or the smooth fabric of a gown, can make readers feel more connected to the scene. For example, "Her fingers brushed against the cool, damp moss clinging to the stones" conveys a tangible experience.

Taste is perhaps the rarest sense used in descriptions but can be incredibly effective when appropriate. Describing the bitterness of overcooked coffee or the sweetness of fresh strawberries can transport readers directly into the scene. However, use this sparingly and only when it naturally fits the context.

Drawing from personal experiences can enhance authenticity in your writing. Think about moments when sensory details left a strong impression on you. These personal anecdotes can add a genuine flavor to your descriptions, making them more relatable to readers. For instance, recalling the salty tang of sea air from a beach trip can lend credibility to a seaside setting in your story.

Active verbs and precise nouns significantly amplify the power of your descriptions. Instead of using passive language, choose active verbs that convey action and atmosphere effectively. For example, rather than saying, "The wind was blowing," opt for "The wind howled through the canyon." Active verbs make the writing more dynamic and engaging.

Similarly, precise nouns enhance clarity and vividness. Instead of generic terms like "tree" or "flower," specify "oak" or "daffodil" to create a more accurate and detailed picture. Specific language invites readers to visualize and feel the setting as the characters do, making the world more immersive.

While sensory details are crucial, avoiding over-description is equally important. Overloading readers with too many details can overwhelm them and detract from the narrative flow. It's essential to strike a balance, providing enough information to create a vivid image without bogging down the story. For instance, instead of detailing every single aspect of a room, focus on a few key elements that set the scene effectively.

Knowing when to show restraint is a skill that comes with practice. Sometimes, leaving space for the reader's imagination can be just as powerful. Strategic sensory details can suggest more than they explicitly state, allowing readers to fill in the gaps with their interpretations. This interplay between writer and reader can lead to a deeper engagement with the text.

Incorporating sensory details effectively requires thoughtful consideration and deliberate choices. Start by layering sensory elements one at a time. Begin with a visual description and then add sounds and smells to enrich the scene. As you write, ask yourself what the character would naturally notice and how these details can enhance the mood and atmosphere of the story.

Consider the emotional state of your characters as well. A joyful character might notice different sensory details than one who is anxious or frightened. Tailoring sensory descriptions to fit the character's perspective can add depth and nuance to your writing. For instance, a character on a peaceful walk might notice the gentle rustling of leaves and the chirping of birds, while one fleeing danger might focus on the pounding of their heart and the threatening shadows.

By practicing these techniques, you'll develop a keen sense of incorporating sensory details that elevate your storytelling. Your readers will find themselves immersed in the worlds you create, experiencing the sights, sounds, smells, touches, and tastes along with your characters. The result will be a more engaging, memorable narrative that resonates on multiple levels.

Concluding Thoughts

As we've seen, world-building isn't just about creating a backdrop; it's about crafting a living, breathing environment that enhances your story. Whether you choose to ground your world in historical research, balance fantasy with realism, employ modular techniques, or collaborate with others, each method offers unique advantages. These approaches help you create settings that feel authentic and immersive, making it easier for readers to get lost in your narrative.

Remember, the setting can be as influential as any character in your story. By integrating sensory details and considering cultural, social, and political contexts, you can breathe life into your worlds and deepen reader engagement. Embrace the adventure of world-building and let your imagination soar as you create places where your characters and stories can truly come to life.

Chapter 4: Plotting Your Story—From Ideas to Outline

Plotting your story is an essential step that transforms raw ideas into a coherent and compelling narrative. Transitioning from scattered thoughts to a well-structured outline can seem daunting, but it's a process that every writer must master to create engaging stories. Understanding the mechanics of plot structure provides a roadmap that guides your creative journey. It's like having a blueprint for a building; while there's room for creativity and personal flair, a solid foundation is crucial for stability and coherence.

This chapter will walk you through various techniques to help you build that foundation. You'll explore how to identify core themes and messages that give your story depth and purpose. We'll delve into classical plot structures such as the Three-Act Structure, the Hero's Journey, and Freytag's Pyramid, offering you versatile frameworks to shape your narrative. Additionally, you'll discover innovative approaches like nonlinear storytelling to add layers and complexity to your work. By the end of this chapter, you'll have practical strategies for brainstorming and organizing your ideas, ensuring your plot captivates readers from beginning to end.

Identifying Core Themes and Messages

Thematic depth is a critical element in crafting a meaningful and engaging plot. Novice writers often focus on plot mechanics, but understanding and weaving in themes can provide your story with purpose and resonance. Let's explore the foundational lessons for creating narratives that are rich in thematic content.

Defining Your Theme

Understanding what themes you want to explore will guide your writing process. Themes are the underlying messages or central ideas that give your story depth. They address universal concepts like love, loss, identity, and power, resonating with readers by connecting on an emotional level. Determining your theme early in the writing process helps you stay focused and ensures that your narrative remains cohesive. For example, if you're writing about redemption, every plot point should reflect aspects of this theme, guiding characters towards moments of forgiveness, growth, and change.

Connecting Themes to Character Arcs

Each character's journey should reflect the story's core message. Character arcs are powerful vehicles for exploring themes. As characters grow and evolve, their personal transformations should mirror the thematic elements of your story. For instance, in a story about bravery, the protagonist might start as a fearful individual but gradually becomes courageous through various challenges. This growth not only advances the plot but also deepens the reader's engagement with the theme. Every decision and action taken by your characters should be a step in their thematic journey, reinforcing the story's central message.

Utilizing Subthemes

Introducing subthemes can enrich the story without overwhelming the main message. While your primary theme provides the central focus, subthemes offer additional layers of meaning and complexity. Subthemes can highlight different facets of your main theme or introduce complementary ideas. For example, in a story centered on justice, subthemes like moral ambiguity or the cost of revenge can add depth. These subthemes provide secondary threads that enhance the narrative without detracting from the primary message. Instead of diverting attention, they intertwine with the main theme, offering a richer reading experience.

Evaluating Thematic Consistency

Regularly reviewing whether your plot supports your themes can refine your storytelling. Thematic consistency ensures that all parts of your narrative work together harmoniously. Take time to evaluate each scene, dialogue, and character interaction to see if they align with your chosen theme. Inconsistencies can weaken the impact of your story and confuse readers. For instance, if your theme is about the importance of honesty, but your protagonist frequently lies without consequence, it can undermine your message. Maintaining thematic consistency requires meticulous planning and ongoing assessment, helping your story remain focused and compelling.

Exploring Classical Plot Structures

Understanding classical plot structures is essential for building compelling narratives. These frameworks provide a roadmap, ensuring your story adheres to recognizable patterns that keep readers engaged. Let's dive into some foundational plot structures and how they can serve as blueprints for your writing journey.

Three-Act Structure

The Three-Act Structure is perhaps the most fundamental plot framework. It divides a story into three distinct sections: setup, confrontation, and resolution. This structure helps writers organize their narratives coherently, making it easier for readers to follow the storyline.

1. **Setup:** This is the introductory phase where characters are introduced, and the setting is established. Often accounting for

the first 25% of the narrative, this act sets the stage for the story's primary conflict.
2. **Confrontation:** The second act, or the rising action, comprises around 50% of the story. Here, the protagonist faces obstacles and challenges that create tension and drive the plot forward. It's essential to build suspense and deepen character development during this phase.
3. **Resolution:** The final act, making up the last 25%, brings the story to a close. Conflicts are resolved, loose ends are tied up, and the protagonist's journey reaches its conclusion. This is where you deliver a satisfying payoff for your readers.

Using the Three-Act Structure ensures your narrative has a clear beginning, middle, and end, providing a sturdy foundation on which to build your story (Deguzman, 2023).

Hero's Journey

Popularized by Joseph Campbell, the Hero's Journey is an archetypal story pattern that highlights a protagonist's adventure and transformation. This structure consists of several stages, each representing a different part of the hero's journey.
1. **Call to adventure:** The hero is drawn into a quest or challenge, often reluctantly at first.
2. **Mentor and allies:** Along the way, the hero meets mentors and allies who help them navigate their journey.
3. **Road of trials:** The hero faces tests, enemies, and obstacles that push them to their limits.
4. **Ordeal:** A significant challenge or crisis that serves as the story's climax.
5. **Reward:** The hero achieves a goal or gains new insight, often leading to personal growth.
6. **Return with the elixir:** The hero returns home transformed, bringing back something valuable learned from their journey.

The Hero's Journey allows for profound exploration of human experiences, such as self-discovery and personal growth. This structure resonates deeply with readers, making it a powerful tool for storytelling (Deguzman, 2023).

Freytag's Pyramid

Freytag's Pyramid, developed by Gustav Freytag, is a visual tool that illustrates the rise and fall of tension within a story. This structure breaks down a narrative into five key parts:

1. **Exposition:** Introduction of background information, such as characters and setting.
2. **Rising action:** Development of the main conflict through a series of events.
3. **Climax:** The peak of the story's tension and the turning point for the protagonist.
4. **Falling action:** Events that occur as a result of the climax, leading toward resolution.
5. **Denouement:** Final resolution where the story concludes and conflicts are resolved.

Freytag's Pyramid emphasizes the importance of pacing and the gradual build-up of tension, ensuring that each part of your story contributes to an engaging and satisfying narrative arc.

Nonlinear Structures

Exploring unconventional storytelling methods can lead to innovative and memorable plots. Nonlinear structures break away from chronological storytelling, allowing for greater creativity and experimentation. Some examples of nonlinear structures include

1. **Fragmented narrative:** The story is told out of sequence, with scenes presented in a nonlinear order. This approach can create mystery and require readers to piece together the timeline.

2. **Parallel storylines:** Multiple storylines unfold simultaneously, often intersecting at key points. This can add depth and complexity to your narrative.
3. **Flashbacks and flash-forwards:** Incorporating scenes from the past or future can provide important context and enhance character development.

While nonlinear structures can be challenging, they offer unique opportunities to captivate readers and present stories in fresh, unexpected ways. Writers like Quentin Tarantino have famously utilized these techniques to create dynamic, engaging stories (Bass, n.d.).

Incorporating these classical plot structures can significantly enhance your storytelling skills. Whether you prefer the clarity of the Three-Act Structure, the depth of the Hero's Journey, the pacing of Freytag's Pyramid, or the creativity of nonlinear narratives, each framework offers valuable tools for crafting compelling narratives. Understanding and experimenting with these structures will help you develop well-rounded, engaging stories that resonate with readers.

Techniques for Brainstorming and Organizing Ideas

To create a plot that captivates readers from the beginning, novice writers can benefit significantly from practical brainstorming and organization strategies. This section provides various techniques to foster creativity and clarity, ensuring that the leap from initial ideas to an organized outline is smooth and productive.

First, let's delve into mind mapping, a visual brainstorming technique that encourages the free exploration of ideas. Imagine a large sheet of paper or a digital canvas as your playground. Start with a central concept—perhaps a character or a theme—and draw branches outward to explore related ideas. Each branch can be split into sub-branches, representing different plot points, conflicts, or character developments. This method helps writers see connections they might miss in linear thinking and allows for a wide array of possibilities without immediately committing to one storyline. For instance, if your central idea is "a young girl discovers she has magical powers," branches could include "her training," "her mentor," "opposition she faces," and "the ultimate quest." As you expand each branch, you'll generate a more comprehensive view of potential narrative paths.

Next, consider free writing, another powerful tool for unlocking creativity. Set aside designated time—perhaps ten to fifteen minutes per session—where you write continuously without worrying about grammar, coherence, or structure. The goal here is not perfection but raw idea generation. During these sessions, let your thoughts flow about your story's setting, characters, or critical scenes. If you're writing a fantasy novel, you might end up with a stream of consciousness detailing a mythical world, descriptions of its inhabitants, or snippets of dialogue between key characters. Over time, these unfiltered bursts of creativity can reveal hidden gems and unexpected directions for your plot.

Storyboarding is another indispensable technique for organizing plot ideas visually. Borrowed from filmmaking, storyboarding involves creating a sequence of illustrations or images that represent different scenes or chapters of your story. Each panel should include brief notes about what happens in that scene, who is involved, and any significant details. For example, your storyboard might start with "Scene 1: Protagonist receives a mysterious letter," followed by "Scene 2: Protagonist meets with an old friend for advice." By arranging these panels in specific sequences, you can easily spot gaps in your narrative, identify pacing issues, and ensure a coherent progression from start to finish.

The snowflake method offers another structured approach, where you develop your story from a simple idea to a full-fledged outline step-by-step (Ingermanson, 2012). Begin by writing a single sentence that captures the essence of your story. Expand that sentence into a paragraph summarizing the central conflict, major characters, and primary plot points. Next, turn this paragraph into a one-page synopsis, adding more detail as you go. Continue expanding, transforming the one-page synopsis into a multipage summary, then into detailed character profiles, complex plot twists, and so on. This iterative process ensures that every aspect of the story grows organically from a well-defined core, providing a strong foundation upon which to build.

Mind mapping, free writing, storyboarding, and the snowflake method are all valuable tools with unique strengths. Mind mapping offers flexibility and visual openness, allowing a broad exploration of ideas. Free writing bypasses internal editors to tap into pure creativity, generating a wealth of raw material to sculpt later. Storyboarding imposes order, helping organize scenes and transitions visually, making it easier to see the story's flow. Finally, the snowflake method provides a structured approach to systematically expand a basic idea into a detailed outline.

Incorporating these techniques into your writing practice can facilitate a smoother transition from conceptualization to outlining, making the often daunting task of plotting less intimidating. For instance, starting with a mind map might lead you to a surprising subplot you hadn't considered. A subsequent free writing session could then flesh out this subplot with rich detail. Storyboarding these ideas helps visualize their place within the broader narrative arc. Finally, using the snowflake method can transform these fragments into a cohesive, detailed outline ready for drafting.

Consider an aspiring writer working on a science fiction story. They begin with a mind map centered around "a future where AI controls society." Branches sprout ideas like "political resistance," "AI ethics," "human-AI coexistence," and "technological advancements." Through free writing, the writer explores a scene where the protagonist hacks into an AI mainframe, revealing government secrets. These ideas are then organized through storyboarding, illustrating key scenes like the protagonist's discovery, subsequent chase, and final showdown. The snowflake method rounds off the process, expanding each storyboard panel into detailed summaries, character arcs, and eventual chapters.

Each of these techniques encourages a blend of creativity and discipline, ensuring that your story's skeleton becomes fleshed out with vivid details and logical progression. The key is to remain flexible, allowing ideas to evolve while maintaining a structured approach to organize them effectively.

Bringing It All Together

In this chapter, we've explored essential elements for crafting a captivating narrative. Understanding and defining your theme early in the writing process can provide purpose and resonance to your story. We've looked at how character arcs mirror thematic elements, enriching both plot and reader engagement. Additionally, incorporating subthemes can add layers of complexity without overshadowing the main message, making your story more multidimensional.

We've also discussed classical plot structures like the Three-Act Structure, Hero's Journey, Freytag's Pyramid, and nonlinear narratives to help you build engaging plots. Combining these frameworks with brainstorming techniques such as mind mapping, free writing, storyboarding, and the snowflake method can transform initial ideas into well-organized outlines. By using these tools, novice writers can create stories that not only capture readers' attention but also keep them thoroughly engaged throughout the journey.

Chapter 5: Writing Gripping Opening Scenes

Crafting gripping opening scenes is key to capturing your readers' interest right from the start. A well-written beginning not only hooks the reader but also sets the tone for the entire story. The initial moments should be arresting and intriguing, pulling the audience into the world you've created. These early passages can make or break the connection between the reader and the narrative, making it essential to get them right.

In this chapter, you will explore various strategies to create compelling beginnings that serve as a strong foundation for your story. You'll learn how to establish tone and style that align with your genre, setting the mood for the journey ahead. We'll discuss introducing your protagonist in a way that makes them relatable and engaging without having to dive into the overwhelming backstory. Additionally, this chapter dives into using sensory details to create vivid settings and how to set up an inciting incident that propels the plot forward. By integrating these elements seamlessly, you can craft an opening scene that grabs attention and ensures your readers are eager to continue turning the pages.

The Components of a Strong Opening Scene

To create an engaging opening scene that will captivate readers from the get-go, it's crucial to understand the elements that make such scenes compelling. This section will break down these essential components, providing new writers with a clear framework.

Establishing Tone and Style

The tone and style of your novel's opening scene should set the mood for the entire book. This involves choosing the right words and sentence structure to reflect the genre and the emotional landscape of your story. For example, if you're writing a thriller, short and punchy sentences can create a sense of urgency and suspense. Conversely, a fantasy novel might start with lush, descriptive language that paints a vivid picture of an otherworldly setting.

Guideline: To establish tone and style effectively, consider the following steps:

1. **Identify the genre.** Understand the conventions and expectations associated with your genre.
2. **Choose appropriate language.** Select words and phrases that evoke the desired mood.
3. **Maintain consistency.** Ensure that the tone and style established in the opening scene are consistent throughout your novel.

By setting the appropriate tone and style early on, you signal to your readers what kind of journey they are about to embark on, aligning their expectations with the narrative ahead. As noted in *How to Write an Engaging Opening* (n.d.), avoiding exposition and focusing on high-impact moments can keep readers emotionally invested.

Introducing the Protagonist

Introducing your protagonist in relatable terms is another critical element. Readers need to connect with your main character emotionally to become invested in their journey. This doesn't mean overwhelming them with backstory but rather showcasing the character's immediate situation, emotions, and motivations.

Consider the following example: A young woman nervously prepares for a job interview that could change her life. We don't need to know her whole history right away; instead, we focus on her anxiety, the stakes of the interview, and her determination to succeed. By showing her vulnerability and ambition, readers can relate to her struggles and aspirations.

Introduce your protagonist in a way that highlights their core traits and sets up potential growth or conflict. Remember, it's these first impressions that will either endear the character to readers or leave them indifferent.

Setting the Scene With Sensory Details

A well-crafted opening scene immerses readers into the world of your novel. Using sensory details—sights, sounds, smells, tastes, and textures—can help paint a vivid picture and draw readers into the narrative. Describe the environment in a way that hints at future events without bogging down the scene with unnecessary details.

Guideline: Enhance immersion by using sensory details. Follow these steps:

1. **Engage all senses.** Include descriptions that appeal to sight, sound, smell, taste, and touch.
2. **Be specific.** Use concrete details rather than vague descriptions to create a more vivid picture.
3. **Hint at future events.** Subtly incorporate elements that foreshadow what's to come, creating intrigue and anticipation.

For instance, in a mystery novel, you might describe an old mansion where the protagonist discovers a hidden door. The creaking floorboards, the musty odor, and the dim light filtering through cracked windows not only set the scene but also hint at secrets waiting to be uncovered. This approach keeps readers engaged and eager to explore further.

Setting Up the Inciting Incident

The inciting incident is the catalyst that propels your story forward. It's the event that disrupts the protagonist's normal life and sets them on a path toward their goal. Crafting a compelling inciting incident is crucial for creating a sense of urgency and maintaining strong momentum.

Guideline: Craft an effective inciting incident with these steps:

1. **Create conflict.** Introduce a problem or challenge that disrupts the protagonist's status quo.
2. **Raise the stakes.** Make it clear what's at risk for the protagonist, increasing tension and investment.
3. **Generate questions.** Leave readers with questions that compel them to keep reading to find out what happens next.

In a romance novel, the inciting incident might be a chance meeting between two characters whose lives are completely different. This encounter sparks curiosity, attraction, and perhaps even conflict. In a fantasy novel, it might involve the protagonist discovering they possess magical powers, thrusting them into a world of adventure and danger.

As highlighted in *How to Write a Novel Opening That Hooks Readers* (Matesic, n.d.-a), establishing immediate conflict and creating strong momentum are key. The initial struggle not only piques readers' interest but also gives them a glimpse into the protagonist's thoughts, motivations, and fears.

Bringing It All Together

An engaging opening scene seamlessly weaves together tone, style, character introduction, sensory details, and the inciting incident. The goal is to create a cohesive and compelling beginning that hooks readers and makes them eager to continue the journey.

Let's look at an example: In an urban fantasy novel, the opening scene might take place in a bustling city street at night. The protagonist, a reluctant hero, navigates through the crowd, feeling the press of bodies around him and hearing the cacophony of voices and car horns. He's confronted by a mysterious figure who hands him a cryptic message. The readers feel the protagonist's initial confusion and rising apprehension, setting up the extraordinary adventure ahead. Through vivid descriptions, we sense the city's pulse and the protagonist's unease, all while being introduced to the central conflict that will drive the story forward.

How to Introduce Key Characters and Settings

Crafting a gripping opening scene is essential for hooking readers and ensuring they are invested in your story from the very beginning. One effective way to achieve this is by seamlessly integrating character and setting introductions into the narrative. This subpoint focuses on the strategies you can use to weave these elements into your opening scene, making it both engaging and informative.

Showing Versus Telling

One of the most important techniques in writing is "showing" rather than "telling." This means revealing character traits and motivations through actions, dialogue, and subtle hints rather than outright statements. For example, instead of telling the reader that a character is brave, show them performing a courageous act under pressure. This not only makes the scene more dynamic but also allows the reader to draw their own conclusions about the characters.

Consider the following illustration: Instead of saying, "John was nervous," you might write, "John's hands trembled as he fumbled with the lock, casting anxious glances over his shoulder." This approach paints a vivid picture and pulls the reader into John's emotional state without explicitly stating it.

Utilizing Dialogue Effectively

Dialogue is a powerful tool for defining characters and establishing relationships. By paying attention to how characters speak and interact, you can convey a lot about their personalities, backgrounds, and dynamics, all without resorting to lengthy exposition. Each character should have a unique voice, reflected in their speech patterns, word choices, and mannerisms.

For instance, if one character speaks in short, clipped sentences while another uses elaborate and flowery language, the contrast can immediately tell the reader a lot about their personalities and social backgrounds. Additionally, dialogue can serve to advance the plot and provide necessary information in a natural, engaging way.

Incorporating Backstory Naturally

Introducing a backstory can be tricky, especially in an opening scene where pacing is crucial. The key is to integrate the backstory seamlessly without halting the action. Instead of dedicating paragraphs to a character's past, sprinkle small, insightful flashes throughout the narrative that serve the immediate story. These glimpses should be relevant and support the characters' current motivations and actions.

For example, suppose a character hesitates before entering a dark alley. Rather than launching into a detailed account of a traumatic past experience, you could reveal just enough: "Sarah's pulse quickened, her mind flashing back to that one night five years ago. She shook off the memory and forced herself to move forward." This technique creates intrigue and depth without overwhelming the reader with information.

Creating a Vivid Setting Through Character Interaction

The setting is not just a backdrop—it plays an integral role in shaping the narrative and influencing character behavior. Introduce your setting through the eyes and actions of your characters to make it feel alive and immersive. Show how the environment affects the characters and how they interact with it.

For example, don't simply describe a bustling city street in broad terms. Instead, show a character navigating through the crowd, reacting to the sights, sounds, and smells around them. "Emily dodged a speeding bicycle, the scent of fresh bread from a nearby bakery momentarily distracting her. Street vendors shouted their wares, and she clutched her bag tighter against the swarm of people." This method engages readers' senses and helps them experience the setting firsthand.

Practical Guidelines and Examples

- **Showing versus telling:** Use actions and dialogue to reveal character traits.
    - Example: "Mark clenched his fists under the table, keeping his voice steady despite the anger simmering underneath."
- **Utilizing dialogue effectively:** Define characters through their unique speech patterns and interactions.
    - Example: Instead of "Jake was always sarcastic," demonstrate it: "Nice job, Einstein," Jake smirked, rolling his eyes.
- **Incorporating backstory naturally:** Integrate backstory in small, relevant flashes.
    - Example: "As Mia reached for the necklace, memories of her mother's laugh flooded her mind, comforting her resolve."

- **Creating a vivid setting:** Use character interactions to bring the setting to life.
    - Example: "Carlos navigated the crowded market deftly, greeting each vendor by name, the vibrant colors and lively chatter forming a familiar symphony."

Using Conflict and Stakes to Engage Readers

Crafting gripping opening scenes is vital for capturing and maintaining reader interest from the very beginning. One of the most effective ways to achieve this is by emphasizing conflict and stakes. Conflict introduces tension, while stakes establish what's at risk, both key elements in ensuring the reader's investment in the story. Here's how you can incorporate these elements effectively into your openings.

Establishing immediate conflict by introducing a problem or challenge facing the protagonist sets the stage for an engaging narrative. The conflict doesn't have to be grand—it could be as small as missing an important bus or as significant as thwarting a pending disaster. For example, think about Harry Potter's introduction—the protagonist lives in a cupboard under the stairs and is mistreated by his relatives (Rowling, 1997). This instantly presents a conflict that hooks readers as they root for Harry to escape his dire situation.

Layering conflicts to balance internal and external challenges enriches the narrative. Internal conflicts involve the character's internal struggles, such as fears, desires, or moral dilemmas, whereas external conflicts are challenges posed by outside forces like antagonists or natural obstacles. A well-layered conflict might show a protagonist dealing with self-doubt while also trying to outsmart a villain. In *The Hunger Games*, Katniss Everdeen faces the external conflict of surviving the deadly games while struggling internally with her feelings for Peeta and her determination to protect her family (Collins, 2008).

Raising the stakes early is crucial to convey what's at risk and increase tension. Stakes refer to the consequences that will follow if the protagonist fails to achieve their goal. High stakes make readers care deeply about the outcome because there's something significant on the line. As Tamela Hancock Murray (2019) notes, if the stakes are low, it's hard to maintain reader interest. Consider the impact of high stakes in *The Da Vinci Code*, where Robert Langdon's failure would not only prevent him from uncovering historical secrets but also cost lives (Brown, 2003). Such high stakes ensure that readers are hooked and eager to see how the protagonist navigates the perilous situations.

Generating questions that prompt readers to seek answers adds an irresistible draw to the opening scene. When you create scenarios filled with curiosity and suspense, readers are compelled to turn the pages to find out what happens next. For instance, in *Gone Girl*, the mysterious disappearance of Amy Dunne raises immediate questions: What happened to her? Is her husband Nick involved (Flynn, 2014)? This creates a compelling need for readers to continue the story to uncover the answers.

Guidelines: Effectively integrate conflict and stakes into your writing:

- **Dynamic openings:** Start with an engaging scene that immediately throws the protagonist into a predicament. Instead of easing into the story, drop your characters—and your readers—into the middle of the action. This urgency can be achieved through a sudden event or a pressing deadline that demands quick resolution.

- **Strategic use of description:** Ensure that descriptive elements serve the story by enhancing the tension and stakes. Avoid overly detailed settings that do not contribute to the conflict or stakes. Descriptions should build atmosphere and reflect the protagonist's emotional state, thereby heightening the overall drama.

- **Minimizing exposition:** Show rather than tell the crucial aspects of the conflict and stakes. Use character actions and dialogue to reveal important information instead of relying on lengthy explanations. This keeps the pace brisk and maintains immersion.

- **Finding the right pacing:** Balance fast-paced action with slower moments of introspection to develop internal conflicts and deepen reader investment. Too much continuous action can exhaust readers, while too slow a pace can lose their interest. Striking the right balance keeps the narrative dynamic and engaging.

To illustrate these points further, consider how George Orwell's (1949) *1984* begins with Winston Smith's struggle against the oppressive regime. Immediate conflict is established as he secretly writes in his diary, an act punishable by death. This simple yet powerful start layers political and external conflict with Winston's internal battle of fear versus rebellion. The stakes here are life and freedom, raising intense reader concern. Additionally, the numerous questions generated about the world of 1984 and the fate of Winston compel readers to delve deeper into the story.

Another effective example is J.K. Rowling's (1997) first chapter in *Harry Potter and the Sorcerer's Stone* . The novel opens with a seemingly mundane night in Surrey that quickly turns strange with the appearance of Professor McGonagall and Dumbledore. They leave baby Harry at the Dursleys' doorstep, immediately raising questions about Harry's significance and fate. This blend of an ordinary setting with extraordinary events establishes an intriguing conflict and stakes that keep readers invested.

Final Thoughts

Crafting an engaging opening scene involves a blend of tone, character introduction, sensory details, and the inciting incident. By setting the right tone and style, you guide readers into the world you've created, laying a foundation for their expectations. Introducing your protagonist in a relatable way draws readers emotionally, making them eager to follow the character's journey. Sensory details then immerse them fully into the scene, allowing them to visualize and feel the environment vividly. Lastly, a compelling inciting incident sets the story in motion, hooking readers with immediate conflict and curiosity.

By integrating these elements seamlessly, you create a captivating beginning that promises excitement and depth. As novice writers aiming to hook your readers from the start, focusing on these techniques will help you build strong and engaging narratives. Remember, your goal is to draw readers into your world and make them care about what happens next. With practice and attention to these fundamental aspects, you'll be well on your way to crafting opening scenes that leave a lasting impact.

Chapter 6: Maintaining Momentum—Writing the Middle

Keeping readers engaged through the middle of a novel can be one of the biggest challenges writers face. While the beginning captures interest and the end provides resolution, the middle must maintain momentum and keep the story progressing smoothly. This chapter will guide you on how to recognize and tackle slow points in your narrative, ensuring that your readers stay hooked from start to finish.

In the pages ahead, we'll explore a variety of strategies to keep your middle sections dynamic. You'll learn about introducing surprising twists and escalating stakes to prevent the dreaded mid-novel slump. We'll also get into the importance of varying pacing through sentence structures and scene changes in order to keep your narrative engaging. Additionally, we'll discuss the effective use of subplots and character development to add depth and maintain reader interest. By mastering these techniques, you'll ensure that the middle of your novel is just as compelling as its beginning and end.

Avoiding the Mid-Novel Slump

Maintaining momentum in the middle of a novel can be a daunting task for writers. This part of the book is crucial for keeping readers engaged, yet it often poses challenges as the initial excitement wears off. Recognizing when the story's pacing begins to lag is an essential first step in preventing a mid-novel slump.

As you progress through your manuscript, pay attention to moments when the narrative feels slow or drawn-out. One way to achieve this is by reading sections aloud or having someone else review them. If scenes feel lengthy without advancing the plot or developing characters, it might be time to take action.

Introducing surprising twists or new information at these points can reinvigorate the narrative. Surprises don't always need to be grand revelations—even minor changes can redirect the reader's attention and maintain interest. For instance, a character might reveal a hidden talent or piece of their backstory, adding complexity to the plot. The key is to ensure that these twists fit naturally within the story's progression and don't feel forced (Collier, 2023).

Gradually escalating stakes and conflict is another powerful strategy to keep the middle of your novel dynamic. When early conflicts lead to larger consequences, readers remain invested in the outcome. Introduce new challenges or adversaries that test your characters' limits. This doesn't mean constant action—emotional stakes can be just as compelling. A relationship hitting a rough patch or a character grappling with internal dilemmas adds depth and maintains momentum.

Regular self-checks during the writing process are invaluable. Take breaks to review your manuscript, focusing on pacing. Ask yourself if each scene serves a purpose in moving the story forward or deepening character development. If any scene seems redundant or stagnant, consider rewriting or cutting it. Maintain a balance between fast-paced action and slower, reflective moments to give readers a chance to absorb the story's nuances.

One effective technique to establish consistent pacing is varying sentence structure. Short sentences and paragraphs quicken the pace, creating a sense of urgency, while longer sentences can slow things down, allowing for introspection. This variation keeps the reader from becoming bored and helps control the story's rhythm (Davenport, 2024).

Another valuable strategy involves chapters and section breaks. Ending chapters on cliffhangers or unresolved tensions motivates readers to continue. Starting new chapters with impactful scenes can also recapture interest. For example, after a chapter ending with a mystery, begin the next with a dramatic discovery or confrontation. This ebb and flow of tension maintains engagement throughout the middle of the novel.

It's also important to manage the release of crucial information carefully. Holding back key details can heighten suspense and make readers eager to uncover the truth. Conversely, revealing certain pieces of information can provide relief or set up new questions, maintaining a balance that keeps readers hooked (Davenport, 2024). Flashbacks and foreshadowing can be useful tools here, as they allow you to control the timing of revelations and add layers to the narrative.

As you build toward the climax, increasing the pacing can create a thrilling, urgent atmosphere. However, avoid rushing through significant developments. Ensure that each step toward the climax feels earned and natural, providing a satisfying buildup. Following the climax, a slower pace can allow for resolution and reflection, wrapping up loose ends and giving readers a sense of closure (Collier, 2023).

Maintaining momentum isn't solely about fast-paced action—it's about balance. Mix high-energy scenes with quieter, more introspective moments. Allow characters to grow and evolve, using their development to drive the story. When readers care about your characters, they're more likely to stay engaged, regardless of the story's pace.

To identify pacing issues, regularly review your manuscript and consider feedback from others. Beta readers or critique partners can offer valuable insights into areas where the story might lag. Taking proactive measures based on this feedback can help you refine the middle sections of your novel.

Utilizing dialogue and action effectively can also influence pacing. Fast-paced dialogue can heighten tension, especially in conflict scenes, while slower, deliberate conversations can add depth and foreboding. Likewise, well-described action sequences can accelerate the story's pace, making intense moments feel immediate and compelling (Davenport, 2024).

Employing subplots is another technique to maintain energy. Subplots provide additional layers of conflict and character development, keeping the narrative fresh. They can offer temporary respite from the main plot while still contributing to the overall story. Ensure that subplots are woven seamlessly into the main narrative, enriching rather than distracting from it (Collier, 2023).

Developing Subplots That Enhance the Main Story

Subplots play a pivotal role in enriching the main narrative and keeping readers invested in your story. These secondary threads, intricately intertwined with the main plot, not only add depth but also provide new angles to explore characters and themes, creating a multidimensional reading experience.

First, consider how subplots can parallel or contrast the main plot. A subplot mirroring the primary storyline might highlight similar struggles or aspirations faced by different characters, amplifying the central theme. For instance, if your main character is grappling with betrayal in their professional life, a subplot could explore another character dealing with personal betrayal. This parallel structure helps readers see the broader implications of the theme and creates a more resonant and cohesive narrative. On the other hand, contrasting subplots can provide relief from the intensity of the main plot or offer a counterpoint that deepens the reader's understanding of the primary issues. Imagine a light-hearted romantic subplot running alongside a dark, suspenseful main plot; this juxtaposition can enhance both elements by providing balance.

One effective way to ensure your subplots enrich rather than detract from the main narrative is by regularly reflecting these subplots back onto the main characters. This approach creates cohesion and enriches the narrative framework. When subplots influence the decisions, motivations, or transformations of main characters, it signals to the reader that these secondary threads are integral to the overall story. For example, in a subplot focusing on a secondary character's struggle with addiction, the main character might be driven to confront their own fears or re-evaluate their relationships, thereby tying the subplot directly to their development.

Balancing screen time across subplots is essential to maintain harmony within your story. Each subplot should have enough space to develop but not so much that it overshadows the main plot. To achieve this balance, allocate specific scenes or chapters where subplots come to the forefront, then integrate them seamlessly into the main storyline. This measured approach ensures that subplots enhance the narrative without overwhelming it. As Lynette Eason suggests, transitions involving changes in point of view, new chapters, or shifts in setting can effectively introduce subplots in a way that feels natural and fluid (Eason, 2024). By carefully managing the presence of each subplot, you keep the reader engaged without losing focus on the primary narrative.

Introducing and concluding subplots at key moments is another strategy to maintain relevance and engagement. The introduction of a subplot should feel organic, arising naturally from the events of the main plot. Using foreshadowing can help here; subtle hints or symbolic elements early on can prepare readers for the unfolding of a subplot, making its arrival feel like a logical progression rather than an abrupt shift. For example, a subplot about a character's hidden past can be hinted at through mysterious references or behavior, slowly revealing itself as the story progresses. This method keeps readers intrigued and eager to see how these new elements will impact the main storyline.

Concluding subplots effectively is just as crucial. Each subplot should have its own arc—beginning, middle, and end—and should reach a satisfying resolution before the story concludes. Whether the resolution ties directly into the climax of the main plot or occurs just before or after, it must feel natural and contribute to the overall sense of closure. Leaving subplots unresolved can create a sense of dissatisfaction, undermining the reader's investment in the narrative.

Creating interwoven narratives involves identifying the right moments to introduce and resolve subplots. Look for gaps or unanswered questions in your main plot where a subplot can add depth or complexity. For instance, if there's a lull in the main action, introducing a subplot can keep the reader's interest piqued. Conversely, during high-stakes moments in the main plot, resolving a subplot can provide emotional weight or clarity, enhancing the impact of the climax.

Avoiding subplots that detract from the main story is equally important. Not every idea warrants a subplot, and introducing too many can dilute the impact of your narrative. Ensure that each subplot serves a clear purpose and aligns with the main plot. Subplots should never feel like filler—they should add value by enhancing character development, exploring themes, or providing additional conflict. If a subplot starts to overshadow the main plot, revisit its purpose and adjust its prominence accordingly.

Crafting successful subplots requires a clear understanding of their relationship with the main plot. Shared characters, themes, or settings can serve as bridges between the two, ensuring a smooth transition and cohesive narrative. For example, a subplot involving a secondary character's quest for redemption might intersect with the main plot through shared obstacles or common antagonists. This interconnectedness reinforces the importance of the subplot and keeps the story unified.

Keeping Character Development Consistent

Continuous character development is a crucial element in maintaining reader engagement throughout the middle of a novel. When characters evolve, they keep the narrative dynamic and hold the readers' interest by deepening their connection to the story. Let's look into how emotional and growth trajectories, personal struggles, secondary character interactions, and reflective decision-making play vital roles in this process.

Firstly, having a clear outline of emotional and growth trajectories for your characters helps maintain continuity and consistency. This involves mapping out where each character starts emotionally and what significant changes they will undergo by the end of the story. For instance, if your protagonist begins as a timid individual, ensure that you show incremental steps of courage manifesting through various scenes. A well-crafted trajectory not only tracks these changes but also provides a roadmap for consistent character behavior, preventing any jarring inconsistencies that could disrupt the reader's immersion. Guidelines like character arc templates can be beneficial tools for writers who are new to this practice (Alderson, 2020).

Personal struggles and relatable conflicts significantly enhance character engagement. Readers often relate more intensely to characters facing challenges that echo real-life experiences. As a writer, injecting moments where your characters grapple with inner or external turmoil adds layers of realism to the narrative. For example, an internal struggle such as overcoming self-doubt can be intertwined with an external conflict like standing up to a bully. This dual-layer approach ensures that the character's journey feels genuine and multifaceted. Moreover, when readers see characters dealing with issues they themselves might face, it humanizes the characters and fosters a deeper emotional bond (Alderson, 2020).

Secondary characters are instrumental in revealing layers of the main character and contributing to the overall story depth. These interactions should be more than just filler material—they should add substance to the main narrative. Introduce secondary characters who serve a purpose—whether it's to challenge the protagonist, provide support, or mirror certain traits. For example, a mentor figure can highlight areas where the protagonist needs growth, while a rival can bring out competitive or darker aspects of the main character. As the relationships between the secondary and main characters evolve, they reveal new dimensions and complexities, enriching the primary plot line. It's helpful to create detailed backgrounds for these secondary characters to understand their motivations and how they impact the protagonist.

Each decision made by characters should reflect their growth and drive the story forward. Decision points are excellent opportunities to illustrate character development because they force characters to act based on their evolving beliefs and values. For instance, if your character has undergone emotional growth from selfishness to selflessness, a critical juncture could present a choice between personal gain and helping others. The chosen path should not only be consistent with their developed traits but also push the storyline ahead. This technique keeps the narrative engaging and demonstrates that character actions have meaningful consequences. Regularly reviewing your manuscript to ensure all major decisions align with the character's trajectory can help maintain this consistency.

In addition, integrating elements of the hero's journey can amplify the emotional resonance of your characters' development. This archetypal narrative structure typically involves a protagonist undergoing significant trials, ultimately leading to growth and transformation. By aligning your characters' emotional and growth journeys with this structure, you create a familiar framework that resonates with readers on a subconscious level. The hero's journey mirrors the human experience of overcoming adversity and emerging stronger, which can inspire and encourage readers in their own lives (98thPercentile, 2023).

Furthermore, conflicts within the narrative serve as catalysts for emotional and character development. Conflict drives the characters out of their comfort zones, forcing them to confront their deepest fears and desires. Whether it's a clash of ideologies or an internal struggle, conflict necessitates change. For example, a character might start with a rigid worldview, but through enduring various challenges, they discover flexibility and empathy. These transformations must be illustrated clearly and deliberately in your writing to ensure the development is believable and impactful.

Utilizing vivid imagery and descriptions can greatly aid in depicting these emotional changes. Descriptive prose not only sets the scene but also provides insights into a character's emotional state. Subtle details like a tightening grip or a fleeting smile can convey volumes about what a character is feeling without explicitly stating it. This technique allows readers to infer emotions and connect more deeply with the characters, enhancing their overall reading experience (98thPercentile, 2023).

Moreover, themes interwoven through character arcs can amplify emotional engagement. Universal themes such as love, loss, redemption, and betrayal resonate deeply with readers. By exploring these themes through your characters' experiences, you create a common ground for readers to connect emotionally with the story. For instance, a theme of redemption might follow a character seeking atonement for past mistakes, offering readers a poignant exploration of guilt and forgiveness. The thematic depth adds another layer to character development, making the narrative more compelling and memorable.

To effectively implement continuous character development, consider using tools like a scene tracker. A tracker typically includes essential elements to track, such as character emotional development and change, ensuring consistency and depth throughout the story. Its purpose is to help writers monitor emotional and character development across scenes, ensuring each moment contributes to the overall growth arc (Alderson, 2020).

Final Thoughts

Keeping your readers hooked throughout the middle of your novel might seem challenging, but remember that every twist and turn can breathe new life into your story. By focusing on developing intriguing subplots and ensuring your characters continue to grow, you create a rich, engaging narrative that holds readers' attention. Emphasize your characters' emotional journeys and intersperse moments of high stakes with reflective pauses, allowing readers to connect deeply with your story.

Balancing action with introspection while seamlessly integrating subplots will help maintain a dynamic pace. Use feedback from beta readers to identify any slow spots and adjust accordingly. Craft cliffhangers and powerful scene openings to keep the excitement high and ensure each part of your novel feels essential. With these strategies, you'll not only avoid the mid-novel slump but also deliver a compelling read that keeps readers turning pages eagerly.

Chapter 7: Crafting Satisfying Endings

Crafting satisfying endings is a pivotal aspect of storytelling that can leave a lasting impression on readers. An ending that feels both surprising and inevitable is what every writer strives for, but achieving this balance can be challenging. It's about creating a conclusion that resonates deeply with the audience, tying up loose ends while providing emotional and thematic closure. Whether your story concludes with a twist or a gradual realization, the goal is to ensure the reader walks away feeling fulfilled and reflective.

In this chapter, we'll explore various techniques to help you master the art of crafting endings that are both memorable and meaningful. You'll learn how to identify the natural conclusion points in your storyline, making sure the end feels earned and not abrupt. We'll look into recognizing pivotal moments and understanding character arcs, helping you decide when your story has reached its destined conclusion. Additionally, we'll discuss the importance of maintaining tension and avoiding unnecessary extensions that can dilute the impact of your narrative. By examining classic literature and gathering feedback from trusted readers, you'll gain insights into what makes an ending truly resonate. This chapter is designed to equip you with practical tools and creative strategies to ensure your stories leave a lasting mark on your readers.

Recognizing When to End Your Story

Identifying when to conclude your narrative is an essential skill that every writer must develop. A well-timed ending ensures that the story resonates with the audience, leaving them satisfied and reflective. This section will guide you through recognizing pivotal moments, avoiding unnecessary extensions, reviewing narrative goals, and gathering feedback from trusted readers.

The first step in identifying the appropriate moment to end your story is recognizing pivotal moments. These are the key events that signify the climax or resolution of your narrative. The pivotal moment often comes after a series of developments and obstacles your characters face. It's the point where everything converges toward the story's ultimate goal. For example, in J.R.R. Tolkien's *The Lord of the Rings*, Frodo destroying the Ring at Mount Doom marks the climactic resolution of his arduous journey (Box, 2017). By focusing on such moments, you can naturally lead your story to its conclusion without forcing an abrupt ending.

In addition to recognizing pivotal moments, writers should also examine character arcs to determine when they reach a point of catharsis. A character arc encompasses the transformation or inner journey of your character over the course of your story. When your protagonist has completed their development and achieved their goals, it signals that the story may be ready to end. For instance, Luke Skywalker's decision to trust the Force and destroy the Death Star represents both a plot climax and his character reaching a significant moment of internal growth (Author Learning Center, n.d.).

Another critical aspect of timing your ending is analyzing the buildup of tension and discovering when it peaks. Tension keeps your readers engaged and invested in the story. As the narrative unfolds, tension should rise, leading to the highest point during the climax. Once this peak is reached and the primary conflicts are resolved, it's an excellent indicator that the story should start drawing to a close. Analyzing how tension builds and dissipates can help you decide the perfect moment to finalize your narrative.

Once you've identified pivotal moments and analyzed the character arcs, it's crucial to avoid unnecessary extensions. Prolonged resolution sequences can dilute the emotional impact and leave readers feeling frustrated. To maintain focus, recognize when to cut secondary storylines that no longer serve the primary narrative. Extraneous details can distract from the main plot and detract from the overall experience. Consider stories like George Orwell's *1984*, where the conclusion is concise and direct, leaving a lasting impact without unnecessary detours.

When considering the length and elements of your ending, learning from classic literature provides valuable insights into crafting concise conclusions. Reading a broad range of endings in timeless works can offer diverse perspectives on how to wrap up a story effectively. Classic novels often balance narrative resolution with thematic depth, inspiring modern writers to find their own methods for striking a similar balance.

Reviewing narrative goals is another essential practice to ensure your ending aligns with the initial story objectives. Writers should ask themselves if they have adequately addressed the central theme. Returning to your original goals can provide clarity and direction for the ending. Asking questions like, "Have I conveyed the core message of my story?" can help ground the conclusion in the established narrative framework.

Rereading the first draft to see if the ending diverges from the anticipated direction is an effective strategy for evaluating coherence. Sometimes while writing, the story takes unexpected turns. Reviewing your draft allows you to reassess whether these deviations enhance or weaken the storyline. Ensure that the resolution feels like a natural outgrowth of the plot rather than an artificial closure.

Gathering feedback from trusted readers is invaluable in determining when a story feels complete. Often, as writers, we can become too attached to our work, making it difficult to notice gaps or unnecessary extensions. Trusted peers can provide insights that you might overlook and offer fresh perspectives on whether the ending is satisfying and coherent. Their feedback can pinpoint exactly where the story could be trimmed or expanded to achieve a more impactful conclusion.

Lastly, ensuring that the resolution feels like a natural outgrowth of the plot is critical. The ending should stem organically from the preceding events, providing a seamless transition from conflict to resolution. Forced or abrupt conclusions can leave readers unsatisfied. A thoughtful and well-integrated ending reinforces the themes and messages presented throughout the story, enhancing its overall appeal.

Resolving Main and Subplot Threads

The final act of any story is crucial in leaving a lasting impression on readers. To achieve this, resolving both primary and secondary narrative threads is essential. A coherent and satisfying conclusion comes from carefully intertwining all story arcs, ensuring that no significant thread is left hanging. This task can seem daunting, but there are various techniques to help writers connect story elements effectively.

Mapping narrative threads allows writers to visualize how different parts of their story fit together. By creating a plot map, writers can track character journeys and subplots throughout the narrative. This process helps ensure that every element introduced in the story contributes to the overall arc and finds resolution by the end. For instance, if a subplot involves a character's search for identity, the plot map would highlight key moments where this journey intersects with the main storyline.

While mapping, it's important to identify underdeveloped threads. These might be secondary characters or minor plot points that haven't been fully explored. Recognizing these gaps allows writers to decide whether to expand these threads or eliminate them entirely. Ensuring that each subplot receives attention helps maintain a balanced narrative where every part feels intentional and impactful.

In addition to tracking individual threads, assessing connections between characters can reveal opportunities to highlight how their stories intertwine. For example, two seemingly unrelated subplots might share a common theme or outcome that strengthens the narrative's core message when brought together. By emphasizing these connections, writers can create a more cohesive structure of events that supports the primary storyline.

Plot cohesion goes beyond merely tying up loose ends. It involves discussing how to seamlessly integrate subplots into the larger framework of the story. One approach is to examine how subplots enhance or contrast the main narrative theme. For instance, if the central theme is about overcoming adversity, subplots might explore different facets of this theme through various characters' experiences. Each subplot should serve to deepen the reader's understanding of the main theme while also pushing the protagonist's journey forward.

Avoiding loose ends requires each subplot to impact the protagonist's journey meaningfully. This doesn't mean every minor character must play a major role, but their arcs should feel consequential to the story's resolution. Techniques for integrating resolutions into the climax include tying character decisions and actions back to earlier events or themes, ensuring a natural progression towards the ending. This way, even small arcs find their place in the grand scheme of the narrative.

Crafting a balanced resolution is about providing closure for all significant arcs without overwhelming the reader with too much information at once. Balanced resolution means giving each narrative thread its due conclusion, ensuring no part feels rushed or unresolved. This can be achieved by staggering the resolution of different threads throughout the final chapters rather than saving everything for the last moment. For example, resolving a secondary character's arc in an earlier chapter allows more space to focus on the main conflict's climax later.

A thematic consistency is vital for a satisfying conclusion. Resolved threads should tie back into the core message of the novel, reinforcing the themes established throughout the story. This can be done by echoing motifs, symbols, or phrases that have appeared earlier in the narrative. For example, if a story's core message revolves around forgiveness, concluding arcs should reflect moments of reconciliation or characters finding peace with their past actions. This thematic reinforcement helps create a sense of unity and purpose in the story's ending.

Consideration of varied perspectives can refine the narrative's closure. Discussing the story with beta readers can provide insights into whether the ending resonates emotionally and intellectually. Constructive criticism helps identify areas needing clarity or further development, ensuring the conclusion aligns with reader expectations and the story's goals. Gathering feedback from trusted readers can signal when the story feels complete, indicating if all significant arcs have been satisfactorily resolved.

Conflict resolution in storytelling also plays a vital role in satisfying conclusions. Addressing and resolving the central tension or problem within the narrative should bring the plot to a logical and fulfilling end. Whether it's a definitive victory over an antagonist or a more nuanced, bittersweet ending, the resolution should feel earned and meaningful. The climax must be a natural culmination of the protagonist's journey, avoiding any deus ex machina solutions that undermine the story's internal logic (Morton, 2017).

Effective endings also leave a lasting impression. They provide closure and reward the reader's investment in the story with a memorable conclusion. This impact can be emotional, intellectual, or both, resonating long after the book is closed. Crafting such endings involves designing scenes that provoke deep responses from readers by ensuring that the story's resolution is as engaging and compelling as its beginning and middle (Greene, 2024).

Creating Emotional and Thematic Resonance

Generating a powerful emotional impact and thematic depth in story endings is crucial for leaving a lasting impression on readers. To achieve this, focusing on a few key elements can make all the difference: echoing prior themes, showcasing character growth, crafting poignant moments, and designing endings that provoke thought and discussion.

First, let's talk about echoing prior themes. Repetition and reinforcement of established themes throughout a narrative provide a sense of cohesion and closure. When an ending revisits central motifs introduced earlier, it creates a full-circle moment that offers resonance and poignancy. For example, if a story begins with the theme of forgiveness, weaving this theme into the final scenes—perhaps through a heartfelt reunion or an act of reconciliation—can tie the entire narrative together, allowing readers to see the thematic thread clearly and feel its weight.

For instance, consider *The Great Gatsby* , where the recurring theme of the American Dream is revisited in the end. Through the tragic demise of Gatsby, the futility and illusion of his dream are underscored, reinforcing the novel's critical view of American society (Fitzgerald, 1925). This thematic echo not only offers a deeper understanding of the story but also strengthens the emotional impact, leaving readers contemplating the broader message long after they've finished the book.

Next, showcasing character growth is essential for a satisfying ending. Characters must reach a significant point of transformation by the story's conclusion, making their journey worthwhile and believable. This transformation should be evident through their actions, decisions, and interactions. It's important to show—not tell—how characters have evolved from who they were at the beginning.

Take Frodo Baggins in *The Lord of the Rings* . By the end of his journey, he is fundamentally changed by the experience of carrying the One Ring, illustrating his personal growth and sacrifice (Tolkien, 1955). This transformation is shown through his actions and the choices he makes, which resonate deeply with readers, making the ending both powerful and emotionally fulfilling.

Creating poignant moments requires careful attention to detail and a deep understanding of human emotion. These moments are designed to evoke a strong response from readers, whether it's joy, sorrow, relief, or a mixture of feelings. One effective approach is to draw on universal experiences that resonate broadly while making them specific to your characters and story.

A great example is the ending of *Toy Story 3* , where Andy gives his beloved toys to a young girl named Bonnie before heading off to college (Unkrich, 2010). This scene is crafted with such emotional depth, capturing the bittersweet nature of growing up and letting go of childhood. It leaves audiences teary-eyed yet content, demonstrating how a well-crafted, poignant moment can leave a lasting emotional impact.

Lastly, leaving a lasting impression involves techniques that provoke thought and discussion. An effective way to do this is by crafting endings that aren't entirely conclusive, inviting readers to ponder the implications and future possibilities. Open-ended conclusions, thought-provoking questions, and meaningful reflections can keep readers engaged long after they turn the last page.

For example, in the movie *Inception* , the ambiguous ending scene with the spinning top leaves viewers questioning whether Cobb is still dreaming or has awakened to reality (Nolan, 2010). This open-ended conclusion fuels endless discussions and interpretations, ensuring that the story lingers in the minds of the audience, stimulating deeper engagement with its themes and ideas.

When incorporating these elements into your story ending, it's important to balance them skillfully. Begin by revisiting and reinforcing your story's core themes, ensuring they are organically integrated into the final scenes. Next, focus on demonstrating clear and believable character growth. Design pivotal, emotionally charged moments that speak to universal truths and human experiences. Finally, aim to leave a lasting impression by provoking thought and encouraging readers to explore the broader implications of your story.

Summary and Reflections

As you wrap up this chapter, remember that the key to a satisfying story conclusion lies in balancing surprise with inevitability. We've explored how recognizing pivotal moments, understanding character arcs, and managing tension can guide you to the right ending. By honing these techniques, you ensure your story concludes naturally, without feeling forced or abrupt. In the same vein, avoiding unnecessary extensions prevents diluting the narrative's impact, leaving your audience with a strong, memorable finish.

Equally important is resolving both main and subplot threads, ensuring every arc ties back into the core themes you've established. Whether it's through mapping narrative threads or incorporating feedback from trusted readers, keeping a keen eye on plot cohesion helps craft endings that resonate emotionally and thematically. Creating poignant moments and leaving room for reflection will ensure your story lingers in the minds of your readers. With these tools in hand, you're well-equipped to conclude your tales in ways that are as engaging as they are unforgettable.

Chapter 8: Self-Editing and Polishing Your Manuscript

Self-editing and polishing your manuscript are essential skills for any writer. Transforming a first draft into a refined piece of work not only prepares it for feedback from beta readers or editors but also helps you see your story with fresh eyes. This process involves several strategies to help you detach emotionally from your work and view it objectively, which can be incredibly challenging yet rewarding.

In this chapter, we'll dive into techniques that will make your editing journey smoother and more effective. You'll learn the importance of taking breaks to gain a new perspective and how reading your manuscript aloud can reveal hidden flaws. We'll explore the use of checklists to ensure no aspect of your writing is overlooked, and how involving friends or fellow writers can provide invaluable insights. Additionally, you'll gain tips on maintaining a balance between external input and your own creative vision. By the end of this chapter, you'll have a toolbox of strategies ready to transform your rough draft into a polished manuscript.

Approaching Your Manuscript Objectively

In the process of self-editing and polishing your manuscript, one key aspect is detaching emotionally from your work. This crucial step allows you to view your manuscript with a critical eye, facilitating constructive revisions. Emotional attachment can blind you to flaws in your writing; thus, learning to create some emotional distance is vital for effective self-editing.

One effective strategy for gaining this perspective is taking a break from your manuscript. After completing your first draft, set it aside for a period–this could be a few days, weeks, or even longer, depending on your schedule. This "cooling-off" period gives your mind a chance to refresh. When you return to your work, you'll see it through new eyes, making it easier to spot inconsistencies, plot holes, or areas where the narrative drags. The time away allows you to divorce yourself from the immediate pride and emotional investment, fostering a more objective approach.

Another useful technique is reading your manuscript aloud. Hearing your words rather than just seeing them engages different cognitive processes. Reading aloud can reveal awkward phrasing, unnatural dialogue, and cadence issues that you might miss when reading silently. For instance, sentences that look fine on the page might sound clunky or overly complex when spoken. This practice not only helps in identifying such issues but also aids in refining the rhythm and flow of your prose. If you find certain sections difficult to read without stumbling, those are likely candidates for revision.

Utilizing checklists can further streamline the editing process and ensure no vital elements are overlooked. Checklists provide a systematic way to approach revisions, breaking down the daunting task into manageable chunks. Items on these lists might include checking for consistent character behavior, ensuring settings are vividly described, verifying plot points, and looking out for common grammatical errors. By ticking off each item on the checklist, you create an organized and comprehensive approach to editing. This methodical scrutiny ensures that all essential aspects of your manuscript receive attention, enhancing the overall quality of your work.

Inviting a friend or fellow writer to read your manuscript offers an additional perspective. A fresh pair of eyes can catch mistakes or identify weaknesses that you might have missed, regardless of how many times you've read the text. Friends or fellow writers can provide honest feedback on elements like plot coherence, character development, and pacing. They bring their own experiences as readers, which can highlight how different audiences might perceive your work. Moreover, they can offer insights or suggestions that hadn't occurred to you, spurring new ideas or improvements.

Importantly, while receiving feedback, it's essential to maintain a balance between external input and your vision for the manuscript. Feedback should guide you, not dictate changes. As the author, you have the final say. However, being open to criticism is part of detaching emotionally. It's about understanding that constructive criticism is aimed at improving your work, not diminishing your efforts.

Detaching emotionally doesn't mean becoming indifferent to your story. Instead, it involves developing the ability to switch perspectives. Think of yourself as both the writer and the first reader of your manuscript. As the writer, you pour passion and creativity into your work. As the reader, you analyze it dispassionately, focusing on how effectively it conveys its message, evokes emotion, and keeps readers engaged.

Techniques for Line Editing and Copyediting

Refining the language and improving readability in your manuscript involves mastering several technical skills. One essential technique is varying sentence length and structure. When all sentences are similar in length or construction, writing can become monotonous and disengage readers. To keep your audience captivated, mix shorter, punchier sentences with longer, more complex ones. For instance, consider how a short statement like "The night was dark" can be followed by a longer, descriptive sentence: "Stars twinkled sporadically across the sky, casting a faint glow that barely lit the landscape." This variation creates rhythm and prevents your prose from becoming predictable.

Next, trimming excess verbiage tightens prose and sharpens clarity. Unnecessary words can clutter your writing, making it dense and difficult to read. For example, instead of saying "due to the fact that," you can simply write "because." Reducing wordiness helps convey your message more directly and efficiently. Here's a practical tip: After drafting a paragraph, go back and question every word. Ask yourself if each one serves a purpose. This exercise will train you to spot and eliminate unnecessary phrases and redundancies.

Ensuring your tone remains consistent throughout your manuscript is another critical aspect of refinement. An inconsistent tone can jolt readers out of the narrative, disrupting their engagement. If your writing shifts between formal and casual styles without clear intent, it can confuse readers. To maintain consistency, decide on your tone at the outset and stick with it. Are you aiming for a conversational tone? Or perhaps a more formal, scholarly approach? Whatever you choose, ensure it aligns with your audience's expectations and the overall theme of your manuscript.

Advanced editing goes beyond basic proofreading—it demands a meticulous review for grammatical and punctuation errors. While grammar checkers can be helpful, they aren't infallible. Familiarize yourself with common grammatical rules and punctuation guidelines to catch errors that automated tools might miss. For example, knowing when to use a semicolon versus a comma can significantly impact the clarity of your writing. Consistent practice in editing will improve your skills over time.

To further enhance readability, ensure that each paragraph transitions smoothly to the next. Abrupt shifts can disorient readers and disrupt the flow of your narrative. Use transitional phrases or sentences to guide readers logically through your manuscript. For instance, if you're moving from a discussion about character development to plot pacing, a transitional sentence might be: "While well-developed characters are crucial, the pace at which your story unfolds is equally important."

Additionally, be mindful of passive voice. Using active voice often makes writing more engaging and dynamic. Compare "The ball was thrown by John" (passive) with "John threw the ball" (active). The latter is more straightforward and livelier. While passive voice isn't always wrong, using active voice can contribute to clearer and more vigorous prose.

Another key aspect of refining your manuscript is ensuring coherence and unity. Each paragraph should support the central thesis or purpose of your work. Avoid tangents or irrelevant information that might distract from your main points. Staying focused not only clarifies your message but also keeps readers engaged.

Incorporating feedback loops into your editing process can also be incredibly beneficial. After completing a draft, seek input from trusted sources, be they peers, mentors, or professional editors. They can offer fresh perspectives and catch issues you might have overlooked. However, remember to stay true to your voice and vision. While feedback is invaluable, it's crucial to discern which suggestions align with your intent.

Embrace the iterative nature of editing. Rarely is a first draft perfect. Multiple revisions are often necessary to hone your manuscript into its best form. Don't be discouraged by the need for continuous improvement—view each round of edits as an opportunity to refine your craft.

Finally, cultivate patience and attention to detail. Rushing through edits can result in missed errors and overlooked opportunities for improvement. Take breaks when needed to maintain a fresh perspective. Editing is a marathon, not a sprint, but the effort invested pays off in a polished, compelling manuscript ready for your readers.

Using Beta Readers and Incorporating Feedback

Effectively using insights from beta readers to improve your manuscript after the initial draft can be a transformative step in your writing journey. It's important to understand that beta reader feedback is an invaluable resource at this stage, offering fresh perspectives that can highlight areas for improvement you might have missed. Here's how to leverage this feedback effectively.

First and foremost, choosing the right beta readers is critical. Ideally, your beta readers should have a good grasp of your genre. Genre-specific knowledge allows them to provide feedback that's not only relevant but also targeted. For instance, a beta reader who is familiar with the conventions of mystery novels will better understand the pacing and tension required, while a fantasy aficionado might focus on world-building and character development. By selecting readers who are well-versed in your genre, you ensure that the insights you receive are contextual and beneficial.

Once you have chosen your beta readers, it's important to guide them in giving you the most constructive feedback possible. Providing feedback forms or specific questions can be immensely helpful here. Rather than leaving feedback open-ended, ask pointed questions like, "Did the plot keep you engaged?" or "Were there any characters you felt were underdeveloped?" This approach makes it easier for beta readers to focus on specific aspects of your manuscript that you're particularly concerned about. Additionally, structured feedback helps you gather more consistent and actionable insights, as opposed to vague comments that may not be as useful.

As you start receiving feedback, it's crucial to approach it with an open mind. While it might be tempting to defend your choices or dismiss criticism, remember that these readers are offering their time to help improve your work. Encouraging a growth mindset allows you to view feedback as an opportunity to enhance your manuscript rather than a personal attack. An open-minded approach will enable you to extract the most value from the feedback, even if it initially feels challenging to accept.

After gathering all the feedback, take some time to reflect on it before making any revisions. Reflecting doesn't just mean reading through the comments—it involves analyzing the feedback to identify common themes and patterns. For example, if multiple beta readers mention that a particular character's motivations are unclear, it's a strong signal that this aspect needs attention. Grouping similar feedback together can help you prioritize which areas of your manuscript require the most significant changes.

Once you've reflected on the feedback, the next step is to implement the necessary revisions. Begin by addressing the major issues—these often have the most significant impact on your story. If, for example, beta readers found a plot twist unconvincing or a subplot distracting, consider how you can revise these elements to strengthen the overall narrative. After tackling the big-picture concerns, move on to smaller, more detailed adjustments based on the feedback.

Revising your manuscript based on beta reader input can feel daunting, but it's a process that can significantly enrich your work. It's essential to maintain a balance between staying true to your vision and being open to change. For example, if a beta reader suggests altering a character's arc in a way that doesn't align with your vision, consider what underlying issue they are trying to address and find a solution that fits your story. Your judgment as the author remains paramount, but flexibility can lead to improvements you hadn't previously considered.

In some cases, feedback may conflict, with one reader loving a particular element while another dislikes it. When faced with conflicting opinions, consider the rationale behind each perspective. Sometimes, the most useful feedback comes from understanding why a reader reacted a certain way, even if you don't end up taking their specific advice. Remember, the goal is to make your manuscript stronger, so weighing different viewpoints carefully can guide you in making balanced decisions.

Ultimately, using insights from beta readers effectively boils down to a few key steps: selecting knowledgeable readers, guiding them with structured feedback requests, approaching their comments with an open mind, reflecting thoroughly on the feedback received, and making thoughtful revisions. Embracing this process will not only improve your current manuscript but also enhance your skills as a writer, preparing you for future projects.

Summary and Reflections

As you wrap up this chapter, remember that revising your manuscript is a journey of refinement. You've learned valuable strategies to detach emotionally from your work, gaining the perspective needed for honest self-editing. Taking breaks, reading aloud, and using systematic checklists are your tools for identifying areas that need improvement. By incorporating feedback from trusted friends or fellow writers, you enrich your manuscript with fresh insights while staying true to your vision.

Embrace the continuous process of refining through editing with patience and attention to detail. Tightening your prose, maintaining a consistent tone, and ensuring smooth transitions will make your story more engaging. Don't rush—multiple revisions often lead to a polished, compelling manuscript ready for readers. Each step in this process not only improves your current work but also hones your skills as a writer, setting you up for future success.

Chapter 9: Navigating the Publishing Landscape

Navigating the publishing landscape can be a thrilling yet daunting journey for aspiring writers. The path to seeing your novel in print involves making pivotal decisions about how you want to share your story with the world. In this chapter, you'll discover the intricacies of both traditional and self-publishing options, equipping you with the knowledge to choose the best route for your unique goals. Whether you're drawn to the established networks of traditional publishers or the creative freedom of self-publishing, understanding each avenue will empower you to make informed choices.

We'll explore the distinct advantages and challenges of traditional publishing, including the roles of literary agents, editors, and the broader distribution network that can catapult your book into bookstores and libraries nationwide. On the flip side, we'll examine the self-publishing model, highlighting the autonomy it offers—from creative control over cover design and content to higher profit margins from book sales. This chapter also introduces hybrid publishing models, which blend elements of both worlds, and provides practical guidelines to help you assess your resources and long-term career aspirations. By the end, you'll have a clearer vision of which publishing path aligns with your dreams and how to navigate it with confidence.

Traditional vs. Self-Publishing Options

When it comes to navigating the publishing landscape, understanding the differences and benefits of traditional and self-publishing can empower you to make informed decisions that align with your goals. Let's look at these options and explore what each path entails.

Traditional publishing involves working with literary agents and editors. This route generally offers wider distribution and marketing support, as publishers have well-established relationships with bookstores, libraries, and media outlets. They often handle the logistics of book promotion, including arranging editorial reviews and organizing book signing events. One of the significant advantages is that your book has a place in physical bookstores, improving its chances of being discovered and purchased. However, traditional publishing can be time-consuming. New authors are likely to face multiple rejections before landing a book deal, and even after acceptance, it may take a year or more for the book to hit shelves (Lauber, 2021).

In addition, authors have limited creative control in traditional publishing. Aspects such as the book title, cover design, and editing are often left to the publisher's discretion. This can be frustrating if you have a strong vision for your work. Royalty rates in this arena are also lower compared to self-publishing, typically ranging between 10–15 percent of the book's list price. Moreover, publisher contracts can be complex, often favoring the publisher, so it's crucial to scrutinize the terms carefully to ensure you retain as many rights to your book as possible.

On the other hand, self-publishing allows for complete creative control. You get to make all the decisions regarding your book's content, design, and marketing strategy. This freedom is particularly appealing if you have a specific vision for your project. Self-publishing also means higher profit margins. Unlike traditionally published authors, who receive a fraction of the book sales, self-published authors can keep most of the earnings from sold books (Lauber, 2021).

However, self-publishing comes with its own set of challenges. You will need to handle responsibilities like book formatting and marketing. This includes managing tasks such as creating and updating a blog, building a mailing list, soliciting reviews, utilizing social media, and contributing articles to drive traffic to your book page. It's a lot of work and can take time away from writing.

Additionally, you will likely need to pay for professional services, such as editing and cover design, out of pocket. Another downside is the difficulty in getting your book stocked in physical bookstores since they often don't accept self-published works due to the lack of the option of doing a return (Editage, n.d.).

One of the hybrid models blending traditional and self-publishing offers flexibility and support. These models can vary but might include aspects from both worlds, such as having access to professional editing and design services while maintaining more control over the creative process. While this seems like an ideal compromise, it's essential to recognize reputable hybrid publishers and be cautious of those looking to exploit authors. Some hybrid publishers may charge exorbitant fees without delivering on their promises, so thorough research is vital before committing to any agreements.

To choose the best path, you need to weigh the pros and cons specific to your goals and reflect on your long-term career aspirations. For some, the prestige and broader distribution network of traditional publishing may be worth the trade-offs in time and creative control. Others might prefer the empowerment and financial benefits of self-publishing, despite the additional workload. Here are some guidelines to help you make this decision:

- **Assess your goals.** Reflect on what you want to achieve with your book. Are you seeking wide distribution and bookstore presence, or is retaining full creative control and maximizing profits your priority?
- **Evaluate your resources.** Consider the time, money, and effort you can invest in the publishing process. Traditional publishing might save you upfront costs but will require patience. Conversely, self-publishing demands financial investment and significant personal effort in marketing and promotion.
- **Research publishers.** If leaning toward traditional publishing or hybrid models, research reputable publishers and understand their contract terms. Seek feedback from other authors who have worked with them to gauge their credibility.

- **Think long-term.** Align your choice with your long-term writing career goals. If you envision frequent releases and control over your brand, self-publishing could serve you better. If you're aiming for mainstream recognition and awards, traditional publishing might be more suitable.
- **Seek professional advice.** Don't hesitate to consult with legal professionals or experienced authors to gain insights and avoid potential pitfalls in contracts and business arrangements.

Writing an Effective Query Letter or Book Proposal

Crafting a compelling query letter or book proposal is essential for catching the attention of agents and publishers. The first step involves understanding the key elements of a successful query letter. This includes an intriguing hook, genre clarification, target audience specification, and conciseness in presenting the novel's essence.

The hook should be engaging and give a glimpse into the core of your story. Imagine you have only a few seconds to capture someone's interest; your hook must make them want to read more. Briefly summarize the main plot or conflict in a way that piques curiosity. For instance, instead of saying, "This is a story about love and loss," get specific: "In a world where dreams are traded as currency, one woman must navigate a labyrinth of deceit to reclaim her lost memories." This immediately sets up an intriguing premise that invites further exploration.

Next, clarify the genre of your book. Agents and publishers need to know if your work fits into a category they are looking to represent. Mention whether it's fantasy, romance, thriller, or any other genre. This helps to manage expectations and ensures your query reaches the right individuals who specialize in those areas. If your book spans multiple genres, briefly explain how they intersect, but do so clearly and succinctly.

Specifying your target audience is also crucial. Who will benefit from reading your book? Whether it's young adults, mystery lovers, or historical fiction enthusiasts, providing this detail helps agents and publishers understand where your book fits in the market. A well-defined target audience shows you have thought about who will buy your book, making it easier for professionals to gauge its potential success.

Importantly, keep your query letter concise. Aim to showcase your novel's essence in as few words as possible. Generally, a single page or 200–450 words should suffice. Over-explaining can dilute the impact of your letter, so focus on sharp, engaging language that conveys the heart of your story without superfluous details. Remember, brevity coupled with clarity is compelling (Friedman, 2020).

For nonfiction authors, crafting a professional book proposal is slightly different but equally important. Your proposal needs to define the marketability of your book, present your qualifications convincingly, and provide a structured overview of what your book covers. Start by outlining why your book is needed in the current market and who will buy it. Include statistics or trends that support the demand for your book's topic.

Your qualifications matter too. Include a bio note that highlights your expertise and experience related to the subject of your book. If you have previously published works, received awards, or have a relevant academic background, mention these to establish credibility. For example, if you're writing a diet book and you're a certified nutritionist with years of experience, this information should be upfront.

A structured overview of your book includes a table of contents, chapter outlines, and sample chapters. Each chapter outline should convey what readers will learn and how each section contributes to the overall narrative or argument of the book. This gives agents and publishers a clear picture of your book's layout and content, helping them envision its final form.

Common mistakes in query letters often spell doom for otherwise promising manuscripts. Avoid clichés and generic wording. Phrases like "this book is unique" or comparisons to very popular works without justification can come off as trite or overconfident.

Personalize each query letter—mention why you chose that particular agent or publisher. This can show that you've done your homework and are genuinely interested in their representation.

Errors, both grammatical and factual, can be fatal to a query's success. Proofread meticulously. A typo or awkward sentence structure may seem minor, but it reflects poorly on your attention to detail and professionalism. Utilize tools like spell check and grammar software, or even enlist friends to go over your query letter before sending it out.

Adhering to submission guidelines cannot be overstressed. Agencies and publishers often have specific requirements regarding how queries should be formatted and submitted. Not following these protocols can lead to immediate rejection. Research each agent's or publisher's requirements thoroughly. They might ask for sample chapters, a synopsis, or even certain formatting styles in the email subject line or body. Following these instructions shows respect for their time and processes (Matesic, n.d.-b).

Tracking submissions is another helpful tip. Keep a spreadsheet listing all agents and publishers you've contacted, submission dates, and any responses received. This helps you avoid resubmitting to the same place or losing track of whom to follow up with. Stay organized, and be patient, as the process can take time.

Understanding Contracts and Rights

Understanding the intricacies of publishing contracts and copyright issues is vital for authors looking to protect their work and ensure they retain control over their creations. A typical publishing contract outlines the financial and legal relationship between the author and the publisher, covering aspects such as advances, royalties, termination clauses, and negotiated publishing rights. Let's break down these components so you can better understand what's at stake when negotiating your contract.

Advances are upfront payments made by the publisher to the author before the book is even published. These payments are typically based on the publisher's estimation of the book's potential success. While receiving an advance can be exciting, it's essential to understand that this amount is recoupable against future royalties. This means you won't see additional earnings from royalties until your book has sold enough copies to cover the advance payment.

Royalties, on the other hand, are ongoing payments calculated as a percentage of book sales. These can vary depending on the format of the book (e.g., hardcover, paperback, ebook) and the terms negotiated in the contract. It's crucial to clarify how royalties are calculated and when they're paid out. Some contracts might base royalties on the retail price of the book, while others might use the net receipts after discounts and returns are accounted for. Always look for escalator clauses that increase royalty rates once certain sales thresholds are met.

Termination clauses define the conditions under which either party can end the contract. Pay close attention to these provisions to ensure you're not locked into an unfavorable agreement indefinitely. Look for clauses that allow you to reclaim your rights if the publisher fails to meet certain obligations, such as keeping the book in print or providing adequate marketing support.

Negotiated publishing rights dictate what the publisher is allowed to do with your work. This could include exclusive rights to publish in specific formats or territories, digital rights, and more. Be wary of overly broad language that grants the publisher more control than necessary. For instance, specific language around subsidiary rights—such as adaptations, foreign translations, and merchandise—should be carefully scrutinized. According to attorney Olivia Loftin (2023), understanding these sub-rights can significantly impact the financial success of your book.

One crucial aspect of protecting your work is copyright registration. Copyright safeguards your creative work and ensures you retain exclusive rights to its use and distribution. In the United States, you automatically own the copyright to your work as soon as it's created and fixed in a tangible form, but registering it provides additional legal benefits. Registration makes it easier to prove ownership in court, allows you to seek statutory damages and attorney's fees in infringement cases, and establishes a public record of your copyright claim.

International laws regarding copyright vary, so it's important to understand how your rights are protected globally. Treaties like the Berne Convention help standardize copyright protections across member countries, but there are nuances in each jurisdiction. Familiarize yourself with fair use provisions, which allow limited use of copyrighted material without permission under certain conditions. Knowing these exceptions can help you navigate potential legal challenges while promoting your work.

Negotiation strategies are vital to landing a favorable publishing contract. One key tip is knowing when to seek legal advice. A lawyer specializing in intellectual property or publishing law can provide invaluable insights and ensure that contract terms are clear and fair. They can help identify potential red flags, such as ambiguous royalty calculations or restrictive clauses, and suggest modifications to better protect your rights. Though legal fees can be costly, the benefits of well-negotiated contracts often outweigh these expenses.

Ensuring clarity in your contract is another critical strategy. Don't hesitate to ask questions about any terms or provisions that aren't immediately clear. Practice negotiation skills by role-playing different scenarios where you might need to discuss your contract terms with the publisher. Being prepared and confident during negotiations can lead to better outcomes. Remember, it's not just about getting the best financial deal; it's also about maintaining creative control and protecting your work's long-term viability.

Post-publication rights are another area where authors must remain vigilant. Understanding subsidiary rights, like adaptations and foreign rights, can open up new revenue streams. For example, film or TV adaptations can be particularly lucrative. Consider whether you're willing to grant these rights to the publisher or if you'd prefer to handle them separately through specialized agents.

The choice depends on who you believe will best exploit these opportunities to your benefit.

Subsidiary rights can also include foreign language translations, audiobook versions, and merchandising. By granting these rights, you may negotiate a larger advance, but retaining them can offer flexibility and potentially higher earnings if handled independently. Some contracts feature a "use it or lose it" clause, meaning unexploited rights revert back to the author after a specified period. This can be advantageous if the publisher doesn't have the capacity or intention to maximize these rights.

Reversion rights are equally important, allowing you to reclaim your rights under certain conditions. If your book goes out of print or the publisher fails to meet sales targets, you should have the option to revert the rights back to yourself. This ensures that your work doesn't languish under a contract without being actively marketed or distributed.

Final Thoughts

Understanding the steps to prepare your novel for submission or self-publishing is essential in navigating the publishing landscape. We've explored both traditional and self-publishing routes, highlighting their unique advantages and challenges. Traditional publishing offers wider distribution and marketing support but often involves limited creative control and lower royalty rates. On the other hand, self-publishing provides complete creative freedom and higher profit margins but requires significant effort in handling responsibilities like formatting and marketing.

Choosing the best path depends on your specific goals and resources. Whether you seek the prestige and broader network of traditional publishing or the empowerment and financial benefits of self-publishing, it's crucial to weigh the pros and cons carefully. Assess your long-term career aspirations, research reputable publishers if considering a hybrid model, and don't hesitate to seek professional advice to avoid potential pitfalls. By taking these steps, you'll be better equipped to make informed decisions that align with your vision and objectives as a writer.

Chapter 10: Staying Motivated and Productive

Staying motivated and productive during your writing journey can feel like a daunting task, especially when you're working on your first novel. As the days turn into weeks and your word count inches upward, it's easy to feel overwhelmed or question whether you have what it takes to see your project through to the end. But fear not! This chapter is designed to equip you with the tools and techniques necessary to maintain long-term motivation and consistent progress. Building on the foundations we've touched upon in previous chapters, we'll now dive deeper into the strategies that will help you stay the course.

In this chapter, we'll explore various strategies to keep your momentum going strong. You'll learn how to set realistic goals using the SMART criteria and why breaking down your writing process into manageable milestones is crucial. We'll also dig into daily writing targets, time-blocking methods, and reflective practices that help assess your progress and adjust your plans as needed. By incorporating these techniques into your routine, you'll build a sustainable writing habit that not only keeps you motivated but also boosts your productivity along the way. Whether you're new to writing or looking to refine your approach, this chapter will provide you with actionable insights to stay inspired and focused on your writing journey.

Setting Realistic Goals and Milestones

Setting goals is a vital aspect of staying motivated and productive on your writing journey. When you break down the abstract idea of "writing a novel" into actionable steps, it becomes much more manageable and less intimidating. Let's dive into some effective strategies to help you set achievable goals that will keep you motivated and create a clear roadmap for your writing journey.

One powerful technique for goal-setting is using SMART goals. SMART stands for Specific, Measurable, Achievable, Relevant, and Time-bound. Setting goals with these criteria in mind helps you clarify your objectives and track your progress.

- **Specific:** Your goals need to be clear and specific. Instead of saying, "I want to write more," specify how much you want to write. For example, "I want to write 500 words daily on my novel." This specificity removes any ambiguity and sets a clear direction for your efforts.
- **Measurable:** Ensure your goals are measurable so you can track your progress. Instead of a vague goal like "Improve my writing skills," a measurable goal would be, "Read three books on writing techniques this month." By quantifying your goal, you make it easier to see your progress and stay motivated.
- **Achievable:** While it's great to dream big, your goals should still be realistic and attainable. If you're new to writing, setting a goal to write an entire novel in a month might be overwhelming. Start with smaller, more manageable goals, such as writing one chapter a week.
- **Relevant:** Your goals should align with your broader writing ambitions. Ask yourself why this goal matters to you. If your ultimate aim is to publish a novel, relevant goals might include completing a first draft or developing a consistent writing habit.
- **Time-bound:** Assign deadlines to your goals. A timeline creates a sense of urgency and fosters accountability. For instance, "Finish the first draft of my novel by December 31st." Time-bound goals help keep you on track and prevent procrastination (Boogaard, 2023).

Another effective strategy involves breaking down the writing process into key milestones. These milestones act as markers of progress and provide a sense of accomplishment along the way. For example, milestones could include completing an outline, writing the first three chapters, or reaching the halfway point of your manuscript. Celebrating these milestones acknowledges your progress and keeps your motivation high. Seeing tangible progress can fuel your determination to continue.

Daily writing targets are another excellent tool to promote consistency. Setting a daily word count target—say, 500 or 1,000 words—can make a huge difference. Doing this helps reinforce writing as a habit. Allocating specific time blocks for writing each day ensures that you prioritize your craft amid other commitments. Writers often find that designated writing times, whether early morning, during lunch breaks, or late at night, help maintain regularity. Consistency in writing is crucial—it turns writing from a sporadic activity into a daily routine. As many seasoned writers suggest, making writing a nonnegotiable part of your day can significantly boost productivity (Bunting, n.d.).

Reflective practices are also essential for maintaining long-term motivation. Periodically reflecting on your achievements and setbacks offers valuable insights into what strategies work best for you. Reflection allows you to assess your progress, identify obstacles, and adjust your plans accordingly. Consider keeping a journal where you document your writing experiences. Reflecting on past successes can reignite your enthusiasm when you face challenges. Also, evaluating your setbacks can help you understand what went wrong and how to avoid similar pitfalls in the future.

For instance, if you find that you're consistently missing your daily word count targets, reflection might reveal that you need to adjust your writing schedule or minimize distractions. On the other hand, looking back at the days when you exceeded your targets can highlight the conditions that led to those productive sessions, which you can then try to replicate more often.

Incorporating these reflective practices into your routine can be incredibly rewarding. They not only help you appreciate your progress but also encourage continuous improvement. By regularly analyzing your writing journey, you can fine-tune your approach, ensuring that you stay motivated and productive over the long haul (Bunting, n.d.).

Let's revisit the guidelines provided:

- **SMART goals**
  - **Specific:** Clearly define what you want to achieve.
  - **Measurable:** Quantify your goals to track progress.
  - **Achievable:** Set realistic and attainable goals.
  - **Relevant:** Ensure your goals align with your overall writing ambitions.
  - **Time-bound:** Assign deadlines to create urgency and accountability.
- **Milestone markers**
  - Break down the writing process into key milestones.
  - Celebrate each milestone to acknowledge progress and boost motivation.
- **Daily writing targets**
  - Set a daily word count target.
  - Allocate specific time blocks for writing to reinforce the habit.
- **Reflective practices**
  - Periodically reflect on personal achievements and setbacks.
  - Keep a journal to document your writing experiences.

Balancing Writing With Other Responsibilities

Finding the perfect balance between writing and daily life responsibilities is crucial for aspiring writers. It helps maintain productivity without feeling overwhelmed. Let's explore some practical techniques to find this harmony.

Prioritization Techniques

Balancing writing with other commitments starts with effective prioritization. Identifying what needs immediate attention versus what can wait is key. You can start by listing your tasks and categorizing them based on urgency and importance. This way, you allocate time more efficiently and ensure that writing remains a priority without neglecting other responsibilities.

For example, consider using the Eisenhower Matrix. This technique involves dividing tasks into four quadrants: urgent and important, important but not urgent, urgent but not important, and neither urgent nor important. By focusing on tasks in the first two quadrants, you can ensure that your most critical duties are completed while still dedicating significant time to your writing.

Time Blocking

Time blocking is an excellent strategy to ensure dedicated periods for writing amid a busy schedule. By allocating specific blocks of time each day for writing, you create a structured approach that enhances focus and reduces procrastination. This method can help you carve out uninterrupted time, allowing you to dive deep into your creative process.

To implement time blocking, choose a calendar or scheduling tool that works best for you. Block out periods specifically for writing and treat these times as nonnegotiable appointments. During these blocks, minimize distractions by turning off notifications and setting boundaries with those around you. Over time, you'll establish a routine that fosters consistent progress.

A useful variation of time blocking is the Pomodoro Technique, which involves working in 25-minute intervals followed by short breaks. This can sustain high levels of concentration and prevent burnout. By combining focused work sessions with regular breaks, you'll find it easier to maintain motivation and energy throughout the day (Bebo, 2024).

Mindful Multitasking

Contrary to popular belief, multitasking doesn't always lead to decreased productivity. When executed mindfully, it can be an effective way to integrate writing into your daily routine. Mindful multitasking involves pairing writing-related tasks with mundane activities, enhancing productivity without sacrificing quality.

For instance, brainstorming story ideas while commuting or cooking can be surprisingly productive. Carry a small notebook or use a voice recording app to capture fleeting thoughts and ideas. This practice turns idle moments into valuable brainstorming sessions and makes the most of every opportunity to nurture your creativity.

Strategic task selection is also essential. Combine high-cognitive demand tasks with low-cognitive ones. For example, outlining a plot while listening to instrumental music or editing chapters during quiet evenings can create a balanced workflow that maximizes output.

Flexibility and Adaptation

While structure is vital, maintaining flexibility in your writing schedule is equally important. Life is unpredictable, and rigid schedules can sometimes add to stress rather than alleviate it. Embracing a flexible mindset encourages resilience and adaptability, allowing you to make adjustments as needed without feeling guilty or defeated.

Start by setting realistic goals and understanding that some days may be more productive than others. If unforeseen circumstances arise, adjust your writing schedule accordingly. Flexibility doesn't mean abandoning discipline—it means being kind to yourself and recognizing that progress isn't always linear.

To cultivate this mindset, periodically review your writing habits and reflect on what's working and what isn't. If certain times of the day prove unproductive, experiment with different writing slots until you find what suits you best. The key is to remain open to change and willing to adapt as you learn more about your personal rhythms and preferences.

Celebrating Progress and Staying Inspired

Acknowledging milestones and maintaining inspiration throughout your writing journey is crucial for long-term motivation. One effective way to sustain your drive is through self-recognition techniques. Celebrating personal achievements, no matter how small, helps boost morale and reinforces your commitment to writing. These celebrations don't need to be grand. Treat yourself to a favorite snack after finishing a chapter or take a relaxing walk when you've completed a productive writing session. By acknowledging these milestones, you highlight progress and maintain a positive outlook on your writing journey.

Finding sources of inspiration is another key aspect of staying motivated. Various external sources can help keep creative enthusiasm alive. Books that align with your genre can spark new ideas and demonstrate storytelling techniques. Music, with its multitude of moods and themes, can transport you into your story's world. Art, whether it's a painting that captures a scene you're trying to write or a sculpture that embodies a character's essence, provides visual stimuli that can deepen your narrative descriptions. Nature offers tranquility and space for reflection. A simple walk in the park might provide the clarity needed to overcome writer's block.

Accountability groups play a significant role in maintaining motivation. Joining or forming a writing group creates a support system where members encourage each other and share constructive feedback. This mutual support can be incredibly motivating, as knowing others are invested in your success adds an extra layer of accountability. Group feedback often brings fresh perspectives, which can inspire new ideas and help refine your work. The sense of community within these groups fosters a motivating environment where writers feel less isolated in their journeys.

Creating vision boards is a powerful tool for visualizing your writing goals and dreams. A vision board is a collage of images, words, and symbols that represent what you aspire to achieve in your writing career. It serves as a constant visual reminder of your objectives and keeps you focused. To make your vision board, gather magazines, photographs, printed images, and quotes that resonate with your writing aspirations. Arrange them on a board or poster in a way that inspires you.

Once your vision board is complete, it's helpful to create entries in a vision board journal. Reflect on why you selected each quote or image and what it means for your vision. Regularly reviewing your vision board ensures it stays relevant and continues to inspire you. Set up reminders to revisit and update your board with new inspiring additions, reflecting on your progress to stay committed to your vision. You can even use digital tools like the Day One app to combine journaling with your vision board, turning it into a beautiful book that captures your journey (Wright, 2023).

As you celebrate achievements and acknowledge milestones, take time to reflect on your vision board. It's important to connect with the emotions and motivations behind each element. Assess the progress you've made and adjust your goals as necessary. Personal growth and writing goals can evolve, so being flexible and willing to update your vision board ensures it remains a true reflection of your aspirations. Celebrating achievements also boosts confidence and motivation, reinforcing your commitment to ongoing progress.

For some, celebrating milestones might mean sharing success with their accountability group or family and friends. Discussing achievements and receiving recognition from others can provide additional motivation. Engaging in discussions about your progress with those around you not only validates your efforts but also encourages continued dedication.

The journey of writing can be overwhelming without inspiration and motivation boosters. Embracing diverse sources of inspiration and maintaining consistent acknowledgment of your achievements form a sustainable approach. Using vision boards and engaging with accountability groups enriches the experience, providing tangible and emotional support.

Summary and Reflections

In this chapter, we've explored various tools and techniques to maintain long-term motivation throughout your writing journey. By setting realistic goals and milestones, utilizing SMART criteria, and breaking down tasks into manageable steps, you can stay on track with your progress. Daily writing targets and time blocking help establish a consistent routine, making the act of writing a nonnegotiable part of your day. Reflective practices, such as journaling achievements and setbacks, provide insight into what strategies work best for you, ensuring continuous improvement.

Balancing writing with other responsibilities requires effective prioritization, mindful multitasking, and flexibility. Celebrating progress through self-recognition techniques and finding inspiration from books, music, art, and nature can keep your creative enthusiasm alive. Accountability groups offer support and fresh perspectives, while vision boards serve as constant reminders of your aspirations. By integrating these strategies, you can sustain your motivation, overcome obstacles, and continue making steady progress toward crafting your first novel.

Conclusion

As we come to the end of this journey together, it's important to take a moment and reflect on everything we've explored. You've learned about the significance of embracing your unique voice, the value of continuous learning and experimenting, the importance of finding a supportive network, and the joy in celebrating your progress. These elements are the threads that weave together the fabric of a successful writing journey.

Every writer has a unique story to tell. Your experiences, perspectives, and voice are like fingerprints—no two are alike. It can be intimidating at first, thinking that your voice might not resonate with readers or that it doesn't fit into the conventional mold. But that is precisely where your power lies. Embracing what makes you unique and infusing it into your storytelling is what will make your writing compelling and relatable. It's this authenticity that readers connect with, making your stories worth telling just the way you see them.

But finding your unique voice is just the beginning. Writing is a craft that evolves over time, much like an artist who continuously refines their skills. Never stop learning. Be curious and remain open to new techniques and styles. Experimenting with different genres and narrative styles can be exhilarating, pushing your creative boundaries and adding layers of depth to your writing. Don't hesitate to step outside your comfort zone, as each new experience enriches your storytelling toolkit.

Writing can often feel like a solitary endeavor, but remember, you don't have to go it alone. Finding a support network can make a world of difference. Whether it's in-person workshops, online forums, or local writing groups, sharing your work with others provides valuable feedback and encouragement during those inevitable moments of self-doubt. In these communities, your dreams become more tangible, and your progress feels more attainable.

Celebrating your progress, no matter how small, is crucial. Writing a book is not a sprint—it's a marathon with many milestones along the way. Each achievement—finishing a chapter, developing a character, getting through a tough scene—deserves recognition. These celebrations fuel your motivation and remind you of how far you've come. Establish attainable goals and rejoice in every step you take towards realizing them.

Throughout this book, we've journeyed through various aspects of the writing process. From brainstorming ideas to crafting well-rounded characters, from structuring plots to navigating the editing process, each chapter armed you with tools and insights to help you grow as a writer. It's essential to internalize these lessons and put them into practice. The path to becoming a proficient writer is paved with persistence, patience, and passion. There will be days of doubt, but these are part of the process. Remember why you started, and let that reason guide you back whenever you feel lost.

Being a writer isn't just about putting words on paper. It's about understanding human emotions, observing the world around you, and connecting dots in ways others might not see. It's about empathy, curiosity, and a relentless pursuit of truth through storytelling. As you continue your journey, allow yourself the freedom to explore, to make mistakes, and to grow from them.

Your writing journey is unique to you, filled with challenges and triumphs that mirror the experiences of countless writers before you. Let these insights inspire and reassure you that you're on the right path. As you close this book and step forward into your own writing endeavors, carry with you the wisdom that your uniqueness is your strength. Continue to learn and evolve, seek out supportive communities, and celebrate your progress. Remember, every word you write is a step closer to becoming the writer you aspire to be. Your story is waiting to be told, and there are readers out there eager to hear it.

So, pick up your pen, open your laptop, or even grab a napkin at the nearest café. Begin your next sentence, paragraph, or chapter.

Trust in your voice, your journey, and the process. The world needs your stories. Here's to the narratives yet unwritten, the characters waiting to be born, and the worlds ready to be created by you. Keep writing, keep dreaming, and most importantly, enjoy every moment of this beautiful adventure.

A Small Ask

Thank you for reading this book! Your thoughts and feedback are incredibly valuable to me and to other readers. Leaving a review not only helps me improve my work but also supports fellow readers in discovering stories that resonate with them. Your insights can guide others in making informed choices and can even impact the journey of this book in the broader literary community. Whether you enjoyed or disliked this book, please take a moment to share your experience—your voice matters!

Leave a review from where you downloaded or purchased this book. Thanks so much!

References

Ackerman, A. (2015, October 15). *Planning a novel: Character arc in a nutshell*. Writers Helping Writers®. https://writershelpingwriters.net/2015/10/planning-a-novel-character-arc-in-a-nutshell/

Alderson, M. (2020, November 24). *Connecting with audiences through character emotions*. Writers Store. https://writersstore.com/blogs/news/connecting-with-audiences-through-character-emotions

Author Learning Center. (n.d.). *How to structure a story: The fundamentals of narrative*. https://www.authorlearningcenter.com/writing/fiction/w/plot-planning/6366/how-to-structure-a-story-the-fundamentals-of-narrative---article

Bass, B.K. (n.d.). *16 Narrative structures to plot a book with*. Campfire. https://www.campfirewriting.com/learn/narrative-structure

Bebo, K. (2024, August 6). *4 time blocking techniques*. Timely. https://timelyapp.com/blog/4-time-blocking-techniques

Boogaard, K. (2023, December 26). *How to write SMART goals*. Atlassian. https://www.atlassian.com/blog/productivity/how-to-write-smart-goals

Box, M. (2017, April 24). *Crisis, climax, and resolution: Story elements for a meaningful ending*. Skyword. https://www.skyword.com/contentstandard/crisis-climax-and-resolution-story-elements-for-a-meaningful-ending/

Bradley, J. (2023, July 8). *The Power of visualization: creating a vision board for personal transformation*. Medium. https://johnbradley1.medium.com/the-power-of-visualization-creating-a-vision-board-for-personal-transformation-6ebaf9072b31

Brontë, E. (1847). *Wuthering heights* . Thomas Cautley Newby.

Brown, D. (2003). *The Da Vinci code: a novel.* First edition. New York, Doubleday

Bunting, J. (n.d.). *Writing goals: how to set meaningful goals for 2021 that you can manage and achieve* . The Write Practice. https://thewritepractice.com/writing-goals/

Carter, T. R. (2023, October 20). What's the importance of theme in fiction?" (exploring themes in your story). *Timothy R. Carter.* https://timothyrcarter.com/whats-the-importance-of-theme-in-fiction-exploring-themes-in-your-story/

Christie, A. (1964). *A Caribbean mystery* . Collins Crime Club.

Collier, J. (2023, June 29). *10 Essential tips for writing a page-turning plot* . SPD StoryStudio. https://spdstorystudio.com/blog/essential-tips-writing-page-turning-plot/

Collins, S. (2008). *The hunger games* . Scholastic Press.

Collins, S. (2009). *Catching fire* . Scholastic Press.

Collins, S. (2010). *Mockingjay* . Scholastic Press.

Costello, D. (2023, September 7). *Crafting subplots that complement your main narrative* . ServiceScape. https://www.servicescape.com/blog/crafting-subplots-that-complement-your-main-narrative

Craig, E. S. (2021, October 4). Want powerful conflict? don't forget the stakes. *Elizabeth Spann Craig.* https://elizabethspanncraig.com/uncategorized/want-powerful-conflict-dont-forget-the-stakes/

Davenport, B. (2024, April 19). *How do authors use pacing to build tension in a story?* Authority Self-Publishing. https://authority.pub/pacing-in-a-story/

Davila, A. (2020, June 24). *Cultivating emotional resonance in your writing* . April Dávila. https://aprildavila.com/emotional-resonance-writing/

Dealing with and overcoming your fear of writing . (n.d.). Writing Master Academy. https://www.writingmastery.com/blog/dealing-with-fear-as-a-writer

Deguzman, K. (2023, July 7). *What is story structure — definition, examples & types* . StudioBinder. https://www.studiobinder.com/blog/what-is-story-structure-definition/

Doyle, A. C. (2003). *The complete Sherlock Holmes* (Vols. 1-2). Barnes & Noble Books.

Eason, L. (2024, May 2). *Weaving subplots through your story* . The Steve Laube Agency. https://stevelaube.com/weaving-subplots-through-your-story/

Editage. (n.d.). *Traditional publishing vs. self-publishing - pros and cons* . https://www.editage.com/book-editing-services-articles/traditional-publishing-vs-self-publishing-pros-and-cons

Editing and proofreading . (n.d.). University of North Carolina at Chappel Hill. https://writingcenter.unc.edu/tips-and-tools/editing-and-proofreading/

Famous Writing Routines. (2022, May 2). *The role of discipline in a writer's daily routine: how to develop a consistent writing habit* . https://famouswritingroutines.com/writing-tips/how-to-develop-a-consistent-writing-habit/

FasterCapital. (2024, June 19). *Time blocking: Mindful multitasking: When time blocking meets efficiency* . https://fastercapital.com/content/Time-Blocking--Mindful-Multitasking--When-Time-Blocking-Meets-Efficiency.html

Feccomandi, A. (2024, January 17). *What is backstory narrative technique?* Bibisco. https://bibisco.com/blog/what-is-backstory-narrative-technique/

Fitzgerald, F. S. (1925). *The great gatsby* . Charles Scribner's Sons

Flynn, G. (2014). *Gone girl.* Weidenfeld & Nicolson.

Friedman, J. (2024, August 9). *The complete guide to query letters* . Jane Friedman. https://janefriedman.com/query-letters/

Gilligan, V. (Creator). (2008–2013). *Breaking bad* [TV series]. High Bridge Productions; Gran Via Productions; Sony Pictures Television.

Gold, J. (2014, July 1). How to use layers to show intense emotions. *Jami Gold* . https://jamigold.com/2014/07/how-to-use-layers-to-show-intense-emotions/

Guest Contributor. (2021, February 18). *Story resolutions: mastering the happy-sad ending* . Writers Helping Writers®. https://writershelpingwriters.net/2021/02/story-resolutions-mastering-the-happy-sad-ending/

Greene, W. (2024, July 24). *Crafting satisfying story endings* . Medium. https://medium.com/@wilbur.greene/crafting-satisfying-story-endings-cccfd9d76201

How to write an engaging opening . (n.d.). Wattpad Creators. https://creators.wattpad.com/writing-resources/sentence-and-scene-structure/how-to-write-an-engaging-opening/

INR. (2018, November 2). *I have noticed that when an author introduces a large amount of characters, those characters are given really quick descriptions and then move onto the next character* [Comment on the online forum post *How to introduce a large amount of characters in the first chapter?*]. Writing Stack Exchange. https://writing.stackexchange.com/questions/39799/how-to-introduce-a-large-amount-of-characters-in-the-first-chapter

Ingermanson, R. (n.d.). *How to write a novel using the snowflake method* . Advanced Fiction Writing. https://www.advancedfictionwriting.com/articles/snowflake-method/

Jarvis, S. (2024, March 29). *Publishing contracts: know your rights and responsibilities* . Spines. https://spines.com/publishing-contracts-your-rights-and-responsibilities/

Julian, S. (2024, June 11). *How to create a consistent writing routine.* Medium; Write A Catalyst. https://medium.com/

write-a-catalyst/how-to-create-a-consistent-writing-routine-1d9de7fb858e

Kauffman, M., Crane, D., & Bright, K. (Creators). (1994–2004). *Friends* [TV series]. Warner Bros. Television.

Lauber, R. (2021, October 26). *17 Pros and cons of traditional publishing vs. self-publishing* . Writer's Digest. https://www.writersdigest.com/getting-published/17-pros-and-cons-of-traditional-publishing-vs-self-publishing

Lee, H. (1960). *To kill a mockingbird* . J.B. Lippincott & Co.

Loftin, O. (2023, February 17). *What authors should know about subsidiary rights* . Romano Law. https://www.romanolaw.com/what-authors-should-know-about-subsidiary-rights/

Martin, G. R. R. (1996). *A game of thrones* . Bantam Books.

Martin, G. R. R. (1998). *A clash of kings* . Bantam Books.

Martin, G. R. R. (2000). *A storm of swords* . Bantam Books.

Martin, G. R. R. (2005). *A feast for crows* . Bantam Books.

Martin, G. R. R. (2011). *A dance with dragons* . Bantam Books.

Martin, T. Y. (2023, March 14). *Backstory is essential to story—except when it's not* . Jane Friedman. https://janefriedman.com/backstory-is-essential-to-story-except-when-its-not/

Matesic, A. (n.d.-a). How to write a novel opening that hooks readers . *Alyssa Matesic* . https://www.alyssamatesic.com/free-writing-resources/novel-opening-hooks

Matesic, A. (n.d.-b). How to write a query letter that gets you a literary agent. *Alyssa Matesic* . https://www.alyssamatesic.com/free-writing-resources/query-letter-for-literary-agent

McAllister, M. (2024, March 12). *8 Tips to becoming a better writer* . Highwire. https://www.highwirepr.com/blog/8-tips-to-becoming-a-better-writer

Morton, R. (2017, July 7). *Meet the reader: Importance of logical conclusions in storytelling* . Script. https://scriptmag.com/features/meet-reader-logical-conclusions-storytelling

Murray, T. H. (2019, September 19). *Stakes versus conflict in your novel* . The Steve Laube Agency. https://stevelaube.com/stakes-versus-conflict-in-your-novel/

98thPercentile. (2023, August 15). *Power of storytelling: Engaging readers emotionally.* https://www.98thpercentile.com/blog/the-power-of-storytelling-engaging-readers-emotionally

Nolan, C. (Director). (2008). The *dark knight* [Film]. Warner Bros. Pictures.

Nolan, C. (Director). (2010). *Inception* [Film]. Warner Bros. Pictures.

Orwell, G. (1949). *1984* . Secker & Warburg.

Quthor. (2024, February 6). Streamlining in a sentence: a step-by-step guide. *Blogs By Quick Creator AI.* https://quickcreator.io/quthor_blog/streamlining-in-a-sentence-step-by-step-guide/

Rowling, J. K. (1997). *Harry Potter and the sorcerer's stone* . Scholastic.

Rowling, J. K. (1998). *Harry Potter and the chamber of secrets* . Scholastic.

Rowling, J. K. (1999). *Harry Potter and the prisoner of Azkaban* . Scholastic.

Rowling, J. K. (2000). *Harry Potter and the goblet of fire* . Scholastic.

Rowling, J. K. (2003). *Harry Potter and the order of the phoenix* . Scholastic.

Rowling, J. K. (2005). *Harry Potter and the half-blood prince* . Scholastic.

Rowling, J. K. (2007). *Harry Potter and the deathly hallows* . Scholastic.

Jordan. (2019, April 1) . Setting the scene: 6 ways to introduce place in stories. *Now Novel*. https://www.nownovel.com/blog/setting-the-scene-create-clear-place/

Severance, K. (2023, May 25). *How to pick a story outlining method* . Medium. https://medium.com/@kimberseverance/how-to-pick-a-story-outlining-method-55a4571adf90

Stover, M. (2024, May 7). *Creating the "write" environment.* Medium; The Freelancing and Writing Source. https://medium.com/the-freelancing-and-writing-source/creating-the-write-environment-5cf3f355e36b

Tolkien, J. R. R. (1954). *The fellowship of the ring* . George Allen & Unwin.

Tolkien, J. R. R. (1954). *The two towers* . George Allen & Unwin.

Tolkien, J. R. R. (1955). *The return of the king* . George Allen & Unwin.

Unkrich, L. (Director). (2010). *Toy story 3* [Film]. Pixar Animation Studios; Walt Disney Pictures.

Urban, D. (2014, April 17). How to be a great beta reader and give helpful feedback. *Diana Urban* . https://dianaurban.com/how-to-be-a-great-beta-reader

Weiland, K. M. (2019a, September 2). *Creating your character's inner conflict: want vs. need* . Helping Writers Become Authors. https://www.helpingwritersbecomeauthors.com/your-characters-inner-conflict-want-vs-want/

Weiland, K. M. (2019b, November 18). *How to overcome fear as a writer and embrace your profound courage* . Helping Writers Become Authors. https://www.helpingwritersbecomeauthors.com/how-to-overcome-fear-as-a-writer-and-embrace-your-profound-courage/

Weiland, K. M. (2022a, August 15). *How to write emotional scenes (without making them cringey)* . Helping Writers Become Authors. https://www.helpingwritersbecomeauthors.com/how-to-write-emotional-scenes-without-making-them-cringey/

Weiland, K. M. (2022b, August 22). *Is your story too complicated? Here are 9 signs* . Helping Writers Become Authors. https://www.helpingwritersbecomeauthors.com/is-your-story-too-complicated/

Wurdeman, A. (2023, September 30). *How to use beta reader feedback: the ultimate guide* . Dabble. https://www.dabblewriter.com/articles/how-to-use-beta-reader-feedback

Wright, K. W. (2023, June 29). *Vision board: Ideas & tips to inspire your goals* . Day One. https://dayoneapp.com/blog/vision-board/

www.ingramcontent.com/pod-product-compliance
Lightning Source LLC
Chambersburg PA
CBHW071720020426
42333CB00017B/2342